who neutered the holy spirit

from doug perry
fellowship of the martyrs

Fellowship Of The Martyrs
118 N. Conistor, #B251, Liberty, MO 64068
www.FellowshipOfTheMartyrs.com
fotm@fellowshipofthemartyrs.com

ISBN: 1463775032
ISBN-13: 978-1463775032

The Bride gets her jewelry, but it's going to hurt to get it on,
and once you're used to it, you're never going to want to
rip it back off again. Heaven is free. HOLINESS is hard!
If not us, who? If not here, where? If not now, when?

DEDICATION

This book is dedicated to Jesus Christ.
In fact, everything I've written, recorded, sung,
spoken or ever done is dedicated to Jesus Christ.
Not that it was all perfect, but that's not His fault.
If you don't like it, blame me, not Him.

I want to take special note of the people who were so
instrumental in helping grow me. Some were used to
encourage me, some were used to teach me patience,
some were used by God to motivate me to find the demon
on them that I might never have seen if they weren't on my
last nerve. Some taught me to endure persecution, even
from the closest friend. Some showed me holiness. Praise
God! They were all a blessing in one way or another and I
really do love them all. (You know which one you were.)

Bob, Nancy, David, Marilyn, Kim, Constance, Stephanie, Ric,
Brad, Keith, Steve, Minnie, Jeannie and Stevie, Andrew,
Rachael, Elijah, Bob, Clare, Gary, Kristi, James, Cindy, Helen,
Sherri, Jen, Dennis, Merri, Joseph, Gary, Cary, Emily, Lili, David,
Yolanda, Suzanne, Tabitha, Josh, Austin, Chris, Candi, Nataliya,
Helen, Ron, Rusty, Josh, Barry, Barron, Glynda, Steve, Bianca,
June, Andrew, John, Lisa, Diane, Larry, Dewey, Jason, Sarah,
Dave, Doug, Michael, Nichole, Dorothy, Tyler, Ky, Kathy, Lizzie,
Patrick, Sharon, Stevean, Randy, Bob, Casey, Amy, Cathy,
Chuckie, Roger, Nils, Ryan, Shelly, Kurt, Sharon, John, Mikey,
Becky, James, Jennie, Angela, Gus, Zach, Jason, Jacob, Greg,
Tres, Danlel, J.R., Tatianna, Patti and Carolyn and HUNDREDS
that I pray will not feel left out but I don't have room to mention.

And a couple million intercessors all over the world pouring
their hearts out and crying rivers on our behalf without
whom I'm not sure how we could have made it this far.
I'm humbled. Please don't stop praying.

I love you all and I'm not going to stop no matter what.

CONTENTS

ACKNOWLEDGMENTS

This book really should not be read all on its own. It is a part of a larger understanding, a series of books written about what is wrong with "church." The statistics are covered in the book, "*The Apology To The World.*" The book, "*The Red Dragon: the horrifying truth about why the 'church' cannot seem to change*" extends on this and shows the supernatural roots and the solution to wipe the slate clean and reboot. The book, "*Rain Right NOW, Lord!*" shows the reality of spiritual gifts, the tremendous need we have for them to be operating correctly – and how to get more of them. And the book, "*DEMONS?! You're kidding right?*" shows how it's under attack and how to defend it. Before we can fix a system, we have to fix each individual, so for personal tune-ups, the book, "*Dialogues with God*" is helpful to learn to hear God better and "*Who Neutered The Holy Spirit?!*" is for those who think God isn't as supernatural as He used to be.

God has been pouring out a lot on Liberty, Missouri. We continue to pray and believe that this will be a refuge, a haven, a training and equipping center. If you're looking for a different kind of "church," something more real and more life-changing, and if the Lord leads, you're welcome in Liberty. When (not if) things hit the fan, if you can make it here, we'll do our best to love you and make a way through all that is coming together.

www.FellowshipOfTheMartyrs.com
fotm@fellowshipofthemartyrs.com

*"Your growth in Christ
is directly proportional
to your willingness
to RUSH HEADLONG
into the refining fire
and give it a wet, sloppy kiss."*

- Doug Perry

PRAYER AND INTRODUCTION

Father God, please open the eyes of our understanding and give us wisdom. Please bind up anything of the enemy – or anything of US for that matter – that would get in Your way. We don't want to hear from Man, we want to hear from You. Please show us what is truth and rule and reign in this time. Please write Your Truth on our hearts. Father, as the vehicle for this writing, I take full responsibility for anything here that isn't pure and true, let any damage done from it be on my head. Let everything that isn't of You drop harmlessly to the ground. Please, Abba? In the mighty name of Jesus Christ, our Lord, Amen.

There are big giant chunks of "Christianity" that seems to think that someone neutered the Holy Spirit. I grew up in one of those chunks and one day I started questioning everything they were telling me – when I saw they weren't feeding the poor, clothing the naked, taking in the poor wanderer, etc., in any substantial measure as a percentage of their budget. I'm pretty sure that's the ONLY stuff on the final "Sheep and the Goats" exam in Matthew 25. Jesus is NOT going to say, "I needed a chandelier and you didn't buy me one. I was desperate for a Power Point presentation and you didn't give me one." Yeah, you get the idea. Don't give me your cheap talk, I want to see your budget. THAT speaks the truth about your priorities.

Anyway, it seems that there is a large chunk of folks that have been taught that the Holy Spirit showed up at Pentecost for the first time, landed on twelve Apostles, did some cool stuff like prophecy and healing and tongues and word of knowledge and delivering demons, and then when the Bible was completed seems to have become nothing more than a beefed up conscience that gently urges us away from things that are bad for us. Like somebody just whacked off all of the Holy Spirit's powerful, multiplication parts! There are many sects of Christianity that never discuss the Holy Spirit at all or completely avoid the Book of Acts for fear that someone might ask an embarrassing question.

Technically called "Cessationists," they think that the Gifts of the Spirit and being able to hear God speak to us stopped (ceased) when the Bible was complete. To support this position you have to go through some serious scriptural gymnastics – the most annoying of which (to me) is that you have to believe that God changes, that the Apostles were unique and special men, that God, in fact, IS a respecter of persons and that the Holy Spirit isn't really as important a part of the Godhead as He used to be. You also have to come to the conclusion that the Great Commission in Mark is not supposed to be in the

Bible and/or doesn't apply to us. And this from folks that insist that the King James Version is the official, infallible, unadulterated Word of God – and Mark 16:14-20 made it in there. So I think they're stuck with it.

My point in this writing is to show the overwhelming evidence that the Holy Spirit was around BEFORE Pentecost, that the Holy Spirit showed up in bigger measure available to ALL people AT Pentecost and that He is available to us in as great (or greater) a measure now as He was to the Apostles. The Baptism of the Holy Spirit is a real thing, it's not the same as salvation and it's absolutely necessary to empower believers to walk in all the full benefits of the Spirit. (But it doesn't have to look the way the Charismatic wing has taught it either.)

So that you know, I don't come at this as a holy rolling Pentecostal. I'm not part of any "Charismatic movement" - I'm just seeking Truth. I was born and bred the son of a Southern Baptist minister and missionary. I'm a stubborn Missouri "Show Me" mule, a businessman, an educator and a pragmatist. I want to know EXACTLY how things work and why and I don't want to take anybody else's word for it. I'm not impressed with cheap talk, I want to see ACTION. What works in the real world can sometimes be VERY different than the way people SAY it's supposed to work. I don't go in for experiences or manifestations or emotional displays – unless it's resulting in radically transformed lives that look more like Jesus.

This is not a scholarly work in the sense that I'm going to go and read the thoughts of dozens of men and synthesize it here with footnotes and a bibliography. I'm going to do my best to just show the Scriptural evidence and present the case as it is in REALITY, not in theory. Science was trapped in a theoretical phase for awhile when men with big brains would sit around a table arguing about how many teeth a horse must have. All kinds of arguments would be proposed based on their understanding of its diet and the mechanics of jaws and whatever other variables or pet assumptions they had. Observational science was born when some genius just got up from the table and went out and found a horse and looked in it's mouth! I'm the kind of guy that has a very low tolerance for sitting around and debating when there is a horse nearby.

The Bible says that they will know us by the word of our testimony. I don't have anything else that I can stand behind reliably except the Bible and what I've seen personally. You may not believe me, I may not be able to document it, but to me it's reality and I can't be talked down – because I went through it and saw it happen with my own eyes. So throughout this writing I might just mix in a "Horse Teeth" reality check from my personal experience here and there. I'll leave it to you to decide if I'm making it up or not. (Hint: I'm not.)

If the Holy Spirit did big stuff BEFORE Pentecost, why do we think that He is unable to do those things AFTER the Bible was completed? If it was just a "dispensation" or for a limited use to spread the Gospel, why is it still happening? Can you come to the conclusion that if people are having dreams and visions and being healed and the Gospel is being spread through unknown tongues, that Satan is doing it? Can a house divided stand? How can that be Biblical? And if it really IS the Holy Spirit doing it and we're denying it or attributing it to Satan, aren't we in danger of blaspheming the Holy Spirit? And Jesus said that was REALLY bad. (Matt. 12:31-32; Mark 3:29; Luke 12:10) Didn't He? The Bible's true, isn't it? If so, you might want to be REALLY careful what you attribute to satan that might really be the Holy Spirit! You know ... just in case.

4

If the Holy Spirit is out there and He is waiting for us to fully appropriate all that He makes available to us to spread the Gospel in power, and we're not doing it – then the blood of all those missed opportunities is on our head. If we have access to weapons and ammunition for this war on evil, but we have been convinced that they're not really there – who benefits most? Yeah, I'm pretty sure the bad guys would REALLY like us to believe that the things which throughout history have most dramatically spread the Gospel are no longer available today. In fact, I'm pretty well convinced that the demons of hell are the ones whispering that doctrine to people. Because I can't figure how Jesus is glorified by a doctrine that says He doesn't heal us or speak to us or do cool things through us anymore. And if we're operating without the full empowerment of the Holy Spirit, then we're running on our own steam. That can't be good. And it plays directly into the enemy's hands.

This is not a side issue of little consequence! If I can hear God better, I want to! If my relationship with Jesus can be deeper, I want it! If I can go from denying Christ when confronted by a bar maid, to preaching my first sermon and 3000 people get saved and the religious leaders beat me and I still won't back down and I go home praising God – I want that! (Acts 5:40-42) Whatever God did to transform Peter from the sissy at the crucifixion to the rock-solid lion at Pentecost, if it's available today, I want it! In fact, if it's available today, the world desperately needs an army of radical, fired-up, fearless rock-solid lions right about now.

This is no small issue. We're talking about whether a THIRD of the God-head changed or not! If the Holy Spirit is God and the Holy Spirit can change, if He got neutered and replaced entirely with a book, then maybe we should

5

be concerned that everything is in a lot more flux than we want to believe. Maybe there's another "dispensation" where the Blood of Jesus doesn't work anymore either! (In fact, some folks are of the opinion that after the "pre-trib rapture" that's exactly what happens! That people Jesus died for can't be saved anymore.)

If He promises us something, like that the power of the Holy Spirit *"is for you and your children and all those far off and ALL those that the Lord calls unto Him,"* but then it doesn't apply to us, how can we feel secure about ANY of His promises? (Acts 2:39) Seems like a bait and switch scam to me. Peter said that what they had just gotten was for everybody. He sold that bill of goods to 3,000 people immediately. It made it into the Bible. But Peter didn't really mean it like that? But God endorsed it and put it in the Bible? Peter could have sure avoided a lot of confusion over the last 1900 years by just telling them that it was for that generation and then it would stop. Wonder why he didn't? It was the Holy Spirit talking through him, right? And the Holy Spirit can't lie, right? So is it for everybody that God calls or isn't it?

Are you getting the importance of this? If some of the Gifts ceased, which ones? If some of the offices ceased, which ones? Who gets to decide which we still have? And if God doesn't speak to us anymore, why not? Do we need to hear Him less? Does He not want to direct all of our paths anymore? (Prov. 3:5-6) Are we not His sheep anymore? 'Cause we're supposed to be hearing His voice. (John 10:27) What about Joel 2 where it says He'll pour out His Spirit on ALL flesh? Have we seen that fulfilled? Could it still be coming? Will we be dogmatically and doctrinally ready to receive it when it happens? (If it didn't already.)

When He said "voice" did He really mean the writings of the Apostles? Maybe when He said "voice" He meant "voice." I'm thinking we ought to take the Bible at face value on that. He put His Spirit in us so that He could write His law on our hearts and we could hear His voice. It's not enough to know the law in general, the Spirit has to show us how it applies to each given situation we face. The Bible says that the Bible is not understandable except by the instruction of the Holy Spirit. So which is more important – the Bible or the Spirit? I gotta go with the Spirit has to come first or the Bible is just a history book. Without the Holy Spirit of the Lord unlocking it to us, we can't search the deep things of God.

Horse Teeth Reality Check

We're going to talk more later about how to hear God. Lots of people that I know hear the Father, the Son and the Holy Spirit – and know the difference. For me, the Holy Spirit is more of a push, more like wind in your sails. He illuminates difficult situations, giving revelation and insight and wisdom. In my own life, it's very rare to have had anything that I would consider a "conversation" with Ruach HaKodesh (the Holy Spirit). The name itself in Hebrew can mean either wind or some invisible moving force. I have heard arguments from some about whether the Holy Spirit is truly a third person of the Trinity or is the moving of God's grace and love and power amongst His people and not properly a "person." The word "Ruach" is also linguistically of the feminine gender. I think the arguments are fairly pointless, and certainly not a justifiable cause for division, since none of us are REALLY going to understand how the "Trinity" works anyway. Seems like a useless quarrel to me.

WAS THE HOLY SPIRIT
AROUND IN THE OLD TESTAMENT?

OK, that's enough of that. Let's get to what the Bible says.

They may not admit it, but there seems to be this stream of thought that thinks the Holy Spirit showed up at Pentecost for the first time and then basically left when the Bible was completed. Or maybe He didn't all the way leave, but pretty much now He's just like a caffeine booster for your conscience. Anybody with a concordance can see otherwise, but I think the enemy has supernaturally blinded people. It's like a cut-and-paste demon that makes them forget certain passages are in the Bible at all!

So, to counteract that, I went through the whole Bible and tried to categorize all the relevant verses about the Holy Spirit. Here are all the people that the Bible specifically says received or were filled with or were motivated by or did something by the power of the Holy Spirit. Surely there were MANY others, in fact none of the prophets could prophecy except by the Holy Spirit, but just so we don't argue about it, these are the verses where the BIBLE specifically says right there that the Holy Spirit had something to do with it. (I'm not saying this is absolutely comprehensive, but it should be enough to make the point.)

I'm going to leave it to you to look them up yourself. If you don't have a Bible handy, try www.BibleGateway.com or www.BlueLetterBible.com . A handy, free computer tool I really like is www.Bible-Explorer.com .

Old Testament people who were filled with the Holy Spirit:

1. Joseph (Genesis 41:38)

2. Bezaleel and Aholiab (Exodus 31:3, Exod. 35:31)

3. Moses (Isaiah 63:14)

4. Seventy elders of Moses (Numbers 11:17)

5. Balaam (Numbers 24:2)

6. Joshua (Numbers 27:18, Deuteronomy 34:9)

7. Othniel (Judges 3:10)

8. Gideon (Judges 6:34)

9. Jephthah (Judges 11:29)

10. Samson (Judges 13:25, 14:6, 14:19, 15:14)

11. Saul (1 Samuel 10:6-10, 11:6, 19:23)

12. David (1 Samuel 16:13, 2 Samuel 23:2,)

13. Saul's messengers (1 Samuel 19:20)

14. Azariah (2 Chronicles 15:1)

15. Jahaziel (2 Chronicles 20:14)

16. Zechariah (2 Chronicles 24:20)

17. The prophets in general (Nehemiah 9:30; Zechariah 7:12; 2 Peter 1:21)

18. Isaiah (Isaiah 48:16; Isaiah 59:21; Acts 28:25-27)

19. Ezekiel (Ezekiel 2:2; 3:24; 11:5)

20. Daniel (Daniel 4:9, 18; 5:11-14; 6:3)

21. Micah (Micah 3:8)

OK, so when did the Holy Spirit first show up? Genesis 1:2. That's darn near as close to the beginning as you can get! And so was the Spirit just sitting on mothballs waiting for Pentecost? What was He doing between Genesis 1:2 and Matthew 1:1?

Things the Holy Spirit did in the Old Testament:

- Moved on the face of the waters (Genesis 1:2)
- Made people speak in tongues ecstatically and/or prophecy (Numbers 11:25-29; 1 Samuel 10:10; 1 Samuel 19:20; 1 Samuel 19:23)
- Complete personal transformation of Saul (1 Samuel 10:6-10)
- Gave David the complete plans for the Temple (1 Chronicles 28:12)
- Made people and kept them alive (Job 27:3, 33:4, Psalms 104:30)
- Omnipresent (Psalms 139:7)
- Wrote the Old Testament (Isaiah 34:16)
- Kills the flowers and the grass (Isaiah 40:7)
- Omnipotent (Isaiah 40:13)
- Prophesied through Isaiah about Jesus being Filled (Isaiah 42:1; 61:1; 63:14)

- Promised to pour out the Spirit on the Church (Isaiah 44:3, 59:21)

- Defended against enemies (Isa. 59:19; Zech. 4:6)

- Picked people up and transported them elsewhere (I Kings 18:12; 2 Kings 2:16; Ezekiel 3:12, 14; 8:3; 11:1; 11:24; 37:1; 43:5)

- Talked to people (Ezekiel 3:24; 11:5)

- Gave dreams and visions (Ezek. 8:3; 11:1; 11:24)

- Transformed and renewed people's hearts (Ezekiel 11:19; 36:26)

- Help people keep His commandments (Eze 36:27)

- Promise to put His Spirit in people (Ezekiel 11:19; 36:26-27; 37:14; 39:29; Joel 2:29)

- Poured out repentance & mourning (Zech. 12:10)

- Spoke through David about Jesus (Psalm 22; Psalms 110:1; Mark 12:36)

- Spoke through David about Judas Iscariot (Psalm 41:9; Psalm 55:12-15; Acts 1:16)

- Spoke to the prophets about the future sufferings of Jesus Christ (1 Peter 1:11)

- Spoke through Isaiah about the future hardness of the people's hearts and their inability to hear the truth (Isaiah 6:9-10; Acts 28:25-27)

Again, that's just a few where the verse specifically gives the credit to the Spirit of the Lord or the Holy Ghost or the Holy Spirit. It should be obvious that He was VERY busy throughout the history of Israel leading up to the New Testament. Surely there are millions of unnamed people of all stripes that heard from the Spirit and were motivated by

Him. That list above doesn't even include Noah and Enoch and Elisha and Gideon and Deborah and Nathan and Samuel and Micaiah and Solomon and Josiah and Nehemiah and Job and Elihu and so many others! None of those people could have done what they did without the Holy Spirit speaking and guiding and directing and filling.

Remember, we're talking about 4,000 or so years here! The Holy Spirit did a lot of stuff, but it seems pretty spread out because the narrative of the Old Testament covers such a giant span of time. But it is the Breath of the Spirit that moves on the waters and puts life into man. It is the Spirit of God that is omnipresent and aware of all that happens and speaks to men as directed by the Lord.

Just to establish the predetermined pattern of Jesus' bloodline required "tweaking" individual lives in ways we can't even imagine! What was required to get Rahab and Ruth and Bathsheba in the lineage of the Christ? How much did the Spirit have to whisper to people, or adjust circumstances, to make it all line up just right? Fourteen generations from Abraham to David, fourteen from David to the Babylonian captivity, fourteen generations from the captivity to the Christ. (Matthew 1:1-17) The exact number of years that Daniel predicted. (Dan. 9:25) What if somebody had been late for their first date? What if Joseph's great, great grandfather Eleazer had died young in battle – or from a bad cold? Yeah, the Holy Spirit was really busy.

Were there any Old Testament warnings about the Holy Spirit? Anything we need to be careful about?

Oh yeah!

Old Testament warnings about the Holy Spirit:

- Better listen to the Holy Spirit and no other (Isaiah 30:1)

- Until the Holy Spirit is poured out there will be desolation (Isaiah 32:15)

- Don't rebel against Him or He'll be your enemy (Isaiah 63:10)

Hmmm. "Don't rebel against Him." That would be like if we denied His presence or authority or said that He didn't really talk to us anymore, right? Would that qualify as rebellion?

What if we said that all the stuff that He might be doing was actually satan doing it? Do you think that would grieve Him? I mean, what if you worked hard and obediently and sacrificially and amazingly – and then had someone attribute all of your labors to your enemy, or to blind chance? That would probably hurt your feelings, wouldn't it? You wouldn't want to do that to a third of the Godhead, would you? I mean, it just seems impolite, at the very least.

You know that God seeks for us to have a servant's heart. That is His economy. He wants us to hear Him and obey without thought of receiving. And God never tells us to do something that He hasn't already modeled for us. He won't ask us to go where He hasn't gone. So what is God's servant heart? The Holy Spirit. The Holy Spirit is the self-less, constantly working, never self-seeking, always giving, always obeying, servant heart of God. We are NOT EVER to worship the Holy Spirit! He does NOT seek worship or glory. All worship and glory and honor is due to the Father. (Phillipians 2:11, 4:20) Even Jesus knew that the ultimate direction of all of our worship and honor is to the Father. He came to glorify the Father, and only said what

He heard the Father tell Him to say. You DO NOT worship the Holy Spirit.

If the Holy Spirit is God's servant heart, tirelessly and selflessly working away to fulfill the Father's plan for us – plans for good and not for evil, to give us a future and a hope – then maybe we should stop spitting on Him.

He's not helpless. The Bible says that if you rebel, He'll be your enemy. I wonder what that would look like? Do you think that maybe He would turn you over to your own reprobate mind or put a strong delusion on you or plug up your ears so you couldn't hear Truth? Maybe He'd turn you over to satan to teach you not to blaspheme. Ouch! I don't think I want to take the chance. I think I'll just be a friend of God and try to stay on the Holy Spirit's good side. Don't mess with God. He doesn't like people taking potshots at His selfless, obedient servants.

WAS THE HOLY SPIRIT AROUND IN THE NEW TESTAMENT BEFORE PENTECOST?

Now this is really fun! Here we have all kinds of neat stuff happening. It all just builds on what happened before. All that cool stuff in the Old Testament is going to get repeated, but it gets compressed down now  into a VERY short window of time. If you see it as a progression, an increasing spiral, and not as a unique dispensation, then there is every reason to believe that it should continue and grow – even exponentially. Like a spiral, what He did before, He's doing again, only more and faster!

Here is a list of the people (that the Bible mentions specifically) that received the Holy Spirit in some measure.

New Testament people who received the Holy Spirit BEFORE Pentecost:

- John the Baptist – from conception (Luke 1:15)
- Elisabeth (Luke 1:41)
- Zacharias (Luke 1:67)
- Mary (Matthew 1:18, 20; Luke 1:35)
- Simeon (Luke 2:25)
- Jesus (Isaiah 11:2; Matt. 3:16; Matt. 12:18; Luke 4:1, 14, 18; Acts 2:33; Acts 10:38)
- The Disciples (John 20:22)

And those are just the direct references. It doesn't include the wise men (Magi) that must have had wisdom from God. It doesn't include Anna or the seventy and the twelve when they were sent out healing people and casting out demons. And all those people being convicted by the preaching of John the Baptist and repenting had to have been having the Holy Spirit speak to their hearts. God pours out the Gift of Repentance by the Holy Spirit. Without that gift from God, no one can really turn from their own sinful nature. So there had to have been LOTS of stuff the Spirit was doing all through this time period.

Things the Holy Spirit did in the New Testament BEFORE Pentecost:

- Revealed to Simeon that he would see the Messiah (Luke 2:26)
- Got Mary pregnant (Matt. 1:18, 20; Luke 1:35)
- Cast out demons (Matt. 12:28)
- Settled on Jesus like a dove in view of everyone (Matt. 3:16, Mark 1:10, Luke 3:22; John 1:32-33)

- Led Jesus out into the desert (Matt. 4:1; Mark 1:12; Luke 4:1)

- Speaks on behalf of God through the Disciples (Matt. 10:20)

- Directed people to go places (Luke 2:27; John 3:8)

- Directed the disciples after Jesus' ascension (Acts 1:2)

So, can there be any doubt that the Spirit was around and kicking before Pentecost? There is also the issue of Jesus selecting and sending seventy and then the twelve disciples out to heal and cast out demons and preach the Gospel. He gave them authority, and we don't know by what process He did it, by laying on of hands or by just speaking it – but you can't drive out demons under your own power, it has to be the Holy Spirit operating through you. So the disciples were saved and baptized and sent out to do miracles well before Pentecost and you can't convince me that you can do that without the Holy Spirit in you!

You can't sustain the argument that they didn't have the Holy Spirit at all until Pentecost. For one thing in John 20:22, Jesus after His resurrection breathes on them and says, "Receive the Holy Spirit." If that was purely symbolic or was prophetic of the time when they were going to receive the Spirit many days later, then why didn't He just say that? In fact, He had already said that, so that would make this uselessly redundant.

The simplest and most literal explanation is usually the best. They needed some peace and patience and wisdom to get through the days following His ascension until the fullness of the empowering of the Holy Spirit came at Pentecost. I think He was giving them a booster of just

17

enough to get them through until then. Certainly in the upper room in Acts 1 Peter is quoting scripture and being a good leader and making a lot more sense than he used to when the rooster was crowing!

There are some verses that people will use to give the impression that the Holy Spirit didn't show up until Pentecost.

John 14:26 (KJV)
But the Comforter, which is the Holy Ghost, whom the Father will send in my name, he shall teach you all things, and bring all things to your remembrance, whatsoever I have said unto you.

John 15:26 (KJV)
But when the Comforter is come, whom I will send unto you from the Father, even the Spirit of truth, which proceedeth from the Father, he shall testify of me:

John 16:13 (KJV)
Howbeit when he, the Spirit of truth, is come, he will guide you into all truth: for he shall not speak of himself; but whatsoever he shall hear, that shall he speak: and he will shew you things to come.

John 7:39 (KJV)
But this spake he of the Spirit, which they that believe on him should receive: for the Holy Ghost was not yet given; because that Jesus was not yet glorified.

People try to say that this means that the Holy Spirit was sent for the first time at Pentecost and that the Disciples didn't receive ANY of the Holy Spirit until then. But that just can't be. Clearly the Holy Spirit was present and active since Genesis 1:2. It must be an issue of quantity or availability to all people, not just an on/off switch. Clearly something MAJOR happened at Pentecost, but it's an error to believe that it was the first time the Holy Spirit made an appearance on the scene. Something definitely happened when Jesus ascended. Somehow it freed up Holy Spirit resources that weren't available to Man previously.

John 16:7 (KJV)

7 Nevertheless I tell you the truth; It is expedient for you that I go away: for if I go not away, the Comforter will not come unto you; but if I depart, I will send him unto you.

It's clear that Jesus was full of the Holy Spirit. I wonder how big His cup was? Maybe He had to <u>leave</u> to free up enough Holy Spirit so the rest of us could get some? Maybe when He ascended to the Father and was glorified He didn't need it anymore, so the Father sent back ALL the Holy Spirit that was filling Jesus' cup – and it was enough to fill everybody for all time!

SO WHAT HAPPENED
AT PENTECOST?

New Testament people who received the Holy Spirit AT Pentecost

- The 120 gathered in the upper room (Acts 1:15, 2:4)

So was that it? They got saved at Pentecost and received the Holy Spirit? The Baptism of the Holy Spirit is the same as salvation? How can that be? They were with Jesus, they acknowledged Him as Lord with their own mouths a long time before this (Matt. 16:16). Presumably somebody had baptized them in water previously (though we're not sure whom). They didn't get the Holy Spirit when they got saved? But they cast out demons and healed the sick?

Do you see the problem? If the promised "Baptism of the Holy Spirit" is the same as the Holy Spirit that we receive at salvation, then the Apostles, who are the foundation upon which the Church is built and the model we are to follow, didn't get saved until the upper room. And how do you account for people that got saved, but didn't get the Baptism of the Holy Spirit until somebody laid hands on them? (Acts 8:15-20) Is there a way that you can get saved, but not receive ANY of the Holy Spirit? That would be bad. We really need to answer that one! There's no way to walk a Christian walk without the Holy Spirit. So if something can happen where we say and pray all the right stuff and really mean it, but don't get the Holy Spirit, it would sure be good to know so that we can avoid that.

But if the Baptism of the Holy Spirit is an empowering event and not a redemptive event, then they can be two separate things and all of this starts to make more sense. In fact, Jesus told them to go into all the world and spread the Gospel. They had been with Him, they had even healed people and cast out demons and preached the Gospel – but that didn't keep Peter from denying Him three times and all the other Apostles from scattering like sheep when the shepherd was struck. But Jesus told them specifically AFTER giving them the Great Commission to NOT go anywhere until the fire fell on them. Had they not seen Jesus? Were they not redeemed? Where they not able to be witnesses? Why wait?

Because they lacked the fire that would transform them and they needed to wait and pray for it – in harmony, all together. And it wasn't a one-time thing, either!

Instances of being REFILLED with the Holy Spirit AFTER Pentecost:

- The disciples again, including Peter and John (Acts 4:31)

- The disciples and all with them again (Acts 13:52)

You see, it's not a fixed quantity. It's not an On/Off switch like you either have some Holy Spirit or you don't. They had increasing quantity. They got filled more than once. The Bible says to "be BEING filled." (Eph. 5:18) That means in a constant state of pouring out on others and getting refilled yourself. And some must have had bigger capacities for the Holy Spirit than others. If you want your SHADOW healing people, you better have a cup like an oil tanker and keep it full all the time! The handkerchiefs that touched Paul's body were healing people! That's a BIG cup of miracle-working, Holy Spirit power there! Not all of them had that big a capacity. I wonder why? Could we get a cup that big? Has that happened since?

So was it just that one time at Pentecost that anybody got that kind of empowering?

Other people receiving the Holy Spirit AFTER Pentecost:

- The seven deacons were either filled at Pentecost or soon after (Acts 6:3-5)

- Barnabas was either filled at Pentecost or soon after (Acts 11:24)

- The Samaritan believers who were saved, but hadn't received the Spirit yet (Acts 8:15-20)

- Paul when Ananias laid hands on him (Acts 9:17; Acts 13:9)

- Gentiles in the house of Cornelius (Acts 10:44-47, 11:15; 15:8)

- The believers in Ephesus when Paul laid hands on them (Acts 19:2-6)

Not to mention the evidence of people in City Churches elsewhere (like Corinth and Rome) that later needed instruction on the Gifts, which must mean they are operating there, which must mean they got the Holy Spirit – and they couldn't have all been in the upper room!

Things the Holy Spirit did AFTER Pentecost:

- Told Peter that Ananias and Saphira had lied (Acts 5)

- Talked to Philip and sent him to teach the eunuch (Acts 8:29)

- Picked up people and transported them elsewhere (Acts 8:39)

- Comforted the Churches (Acts 9:31)

- Gave Peter visions and talked to him (Acts 10:19; 11:12)

- Told about a famine that was coming (Acts 11:28)

- Told other people to tell Paul things (Acts 21:4)

- Mighty signs and wonders (Romans 15:19; 1 Corinthians 2:4; Galatians 3:5)

- Revealed deep mysteries of God to men (1 Corin. 2:10-14; Ephesians 1:17; Ephesians 3:5)

- Dwelt within people (1 Corinthians 3:16; Gal. 4:6)

- Gave spiritual gifts to EVERY person (1 Corin. 12)

- Joins us all in Christ's Body (1 Corinthians 12:13; 2 Corinthians 4:13; Eph. 2:18; Eph. 4:4)

- Prays through our mouths directly to God (1 Corin. 14:2; Galatians 4:6; Ephesians 6:18, Jude 1:20-21)

- Sings through us (I Corinthians 14:15)

- Gives liberty (2 Corinthians 3:17)

- Changes us into the image of our Lord (2 Corinthians 3:18)

- Makes us a temple for God (Ephesians 2:22)

- Established church doctrine (Acts 15:28)

- Strengthens us in our inner man (Ephesians 3:16)

- Spoke through Peter to the elders of Israel (Acts 4:8)

- Gave Stephen a vision and gave strength to endure martyrdom (Acts 7:55)

- Restored Paul's vision (Acts 9:17)

- Told Paul specifically about the last days (I Timothy 4:1)

- Helps purify our souls and love the brethren (1 Peter 1:22)

- Gave John visions and interpretations and spoke to him (Revelation 1:10, 4:2, 14:13)

- Sent messages to the churches (Revelation 2:7, 11, 17, 29; 3:6, 13, 22)

- Will one day raise the two Witnesses from the dead (Revelation 11:11)

- Calls out with the Bride to all them that are thirsty (Revelation 22:17)

- Specifically spoke to the elders in Antioch to send out Paul and Barnabas (Acts 13:2-4)

- Specifically forbid Paul from preaching in Asia - at that moment (Acts 16:6)

- Wouldn't allow Paul to go to Bythinia (Acts 16:17)

- Told Paul to expect persecution and bondage (Acts 20:22-25)

- Made people speak in tongues and/or prophecy (Acts 2:4; Acts 10:46; Acts 19:6)

- Assigns those who are to be servants and shepherds to the Church (Acts 20:28)

- Warned Paul through the Tyrean disciples not to go to Jerusalem (Acts 21:4)

- Spoke through Agabus warning Paul not to go to Jerusalem (Acts 21:11)

This list above includes all of the nine "manifestation gifts" mentioned in 1 Corinthians 12:1-11 – and then some.

1 Cor 12:4-11 (KJV)

4 Now there are diversities of gifts, but the same Spirit. 5 And there are differences of administrations, but the same Lord. 6 And there are diversities of operations, but it is the same God which worketh all in all. 7 But the manifestation of the Spirit is given to every man to profit withal. 8 For to one is given by the Spirit the word of wisdom; to another the word of knowledge by the same Spirit; 9 To another faith by the same Spirit; to another the gifts of healing by the same Spirit; 10 To another the working of miracles; to another prophecy; to another discerning of spirits; to another divers kinds of tongues; to another the interpretation of tongues: 11 But all these worketh that one and the selfsame Spirit, dividing to every man severally as he will.

Just to clarify, the nine "manifestation" gifts listed here are:

Word of Wisdom, Word of Knowledge, Faith, Healing, Miracles, Prophecy, Discerning of Spirits, Tongues, and Interpretation of Tongues

If those things ceased when the Bible was completed (or when the last Apostle died), which ones ceased? Faith? We don't have faith anymore? Or is this some special faith? Like the kind of faith that would let you endure torture and martyrdom and being burned or tortured without renouncing your faith? The kind of super-freaky, over the top, God-inspired faith that you just know that you know that you know that God is in control and everything is going to be OK. And why would that have ended? We don't need that anymore?!

So if I can find an instance, ANY instance of someone AFTER the last Apostle exhibiting this kind of freakish Gift of Faith, wouldn't that prove that it didn't end? That's an easy one. MILLIONS have been martyred and endured devastatingly painful torture and horrible circumstances without denying their faith. Read "Foxes Book of Martyrs" and tell me that Faith like that has ended! Read about Richard Wurmbrand or Brother Yun in China and tell me that the Gift of Faith has ended! Or go watch some of the videos here – www.gfa.org.

What about Word of Wisdom? That's not just saying something wise, that's a pure Godly Wisdom that is spoken for the edification of the Body at the right moment so as to build up and make complete the people of God. Like when Solomon said to cut the baby in half – that was SO pure and clean and right to the very heart of the matter that it had to be God-breathed. (I Kings 3:25) That was a Word of Wisdom. So we don't have that anymore? And we don't need it why? I think we have a desperate shortage of Wisdom in the "church"! How could God be the one benefiting the most by eliminating that one? Surely satan is most glorified when we lack Godly Wisdom. The Bible says that if we seek Wisdom, the Lord will give liberally and without reproach. (James 1:5) Even if

26

we abused it last time, He'll give us more! So how could it be dead? I'm just pretty sure that a demon whispered this theology to somebody because we're to test the spirits and take captive every thought and bring it into obedience with Christ – and I can't figure any way that Jesus would say something like that supernatural, God-given Wisdom and Faith are dead and unavailable to us anymore. That sure sounds like satan to me.

If the only true Wisdom that is available to us today is in the Bible, then why don't all those mega-church pastors stop writing books? If whatever is coming out of them isn't really a spiritual gift, it's just man-made wisdom and the only True Wisdom is in the Bible, then hand me a Bible and shut up.

What about Discernment of Spirits? That's the ability to see into the spiritual realms and accurately tell the good guys from the bad guys. To see what is happening in the "Real" world and know how to address it. Yes, it means that you see demons – but it also means that you see angels. OK, God doesn't want us to have this anymore why? There's not a war between good and evil still going on? We don't need to accurately target and eliminate the enemy? Our battle is not against flesh and blood, but powers and principalities and wickedness in high places – but we don't need to see them or know what they're up to? (Ephesians 6.12)

Hmmm. Who benefits most by a theology that says demons are not real and we can't see them and the weapons of spiritual warfare that were entrusted to us aren't good anymore? Who benefits most by a theology that says that if you talk about satan or demons then you're bringing them glory and denying the power of God? And how come that didn't apply to Jesus? He talked about

27

them all the time! In the war room in the Pentagon, they're never going to talk about Osama Bin Ladin or some other enemy for fear of accidentally worshiping them? This is a WAR!! I want to know where they sleep, what they eat, how they act, how they attack and most importantly, how to crush them into mush! Who benefits most from a theology that says they're not really there or we're not to talk about them? I gotta think it's the bad guys. Are you getting this? I'm just pretty sure that a demon made up this stupid theology because it DOES NOT glorify God in any way for Him to declare a war and then for us to deny we have weapons or intelligence gathering systems or radios to headquarters!

What about Tongues and Interpretation of Tongues? Together they are prophecy and Paul says we're to seek prophecy. (I Corinthians 14:1) Acts 2:38-39 said it was a gift for all generations. This ended why? We don't need to know the languages of other peoples to evangelize anymore? We have over 3,000 language groups on this planet with not a single word of the Bible in their language and no sign on the horizon that we're going to reach them anytime soon. But we don't need supernatural linguistic skills anymore?

So if that ended, but I can show you examples of people who supernaturally were given other languages of Man, what does that mean? Never mind arguing about the stickier issue of whether Tongues (glossolalia) are of men and/or of angels, if we can show evidence of a man supernaturally getting a linguistic package from God to be used to speak to a group about Jesus, that would qualify. And if it happened AFTER the last Apostle died and/or the Bible was completed, then the Cessationists are all wet. Do you see how hard this argument is to sustain? If we can find even ONE instance of ANY of these gifts still

28

being in operation, then they DID NOT end and they're still available to us today. And unless God is a respecter of persons, then they're available to us today in as big a quantity as they ever were to anyone. Jesus Himself said we would do greater things than He did! (John 14:12)

Horse Teeth Reality Check

I happen to be personally acquainted with one lady in South Africa whom the Lord called to preach – in English – but she didn't speak English. So she prayed and the Lord gave her English. You're welcome to email her about it and see if you think she's lying. Her name is Ezette van der Merwe and you can reach her through www.MercyGate.com.

I'm also aware through another friend that runs a small international ministry of a dear friend, and ministry partner of his from Cambodia who was also miraculously given English when they prayed – soon after the Bataan Death March – so that someone could go to the U.S. Embassy and petition for asylum for a group of new Christians.

I've spoken with Wycliffe Bible Translators who don't think it strange at all and have many stories of translators deep in the jungle asking the Lord to help with a particularly hard language and then getting that tongue for prayer and for messages to the church. They may not speak it very well all the time, but the villagers say that when they pray, it's perfect.

I know people that have given messages to other people in perfect Japanese, Russian and other languages they didn't know. Or didn't even know that they were praying loud enough for anyone to hear them, but it was the Gospel being preached to someone next to them on the elevator or something!

When tongues showed up on January 1, 1901 at William Parham's Bible school in Topeka, Kansas, the students there were speaking languages of Man previously unknown to them – including Chinese. It was documented and verified by newspaper reporters. The same at the Azusa Street revival a few years later. Look it up. Read the old newspapers.

Get out of your box and go investigate without your blinders on. (Just in case I'm right.)

How about these?

- 150 AD – Justin Martyr wrote "For the prophetical gifts remain with us, even to this present time." (Dialogue with Trypho, Chapter 82), and "Now, it is possible to see amongst us women and men who possess gifts of the Spirit of God;" (ibid, Chapter 88.)

- 175 AD - Irenaeus in his treatise "Against Heresies" speaks of those "who through the Spirit speak all kinds of languages." (Against Heresies, Book 2 Chapter 4)

- circa 230 AD - Novatian said, "This is He who places prophets in the Church, instructs teachers, *directs tongues*, gives powers and healings, does wonderful works, often discrimination of spirits, affords powers of government, suggests counsels, and orders and arranges whatever other gifts there are of charismata; and thus make the Lord's Church everywhere, and in all, perfected and completed." (Treatise Concerning the Trinity, Chapter 29.)

- circa 340 AD – Hilary of Poitiers wrote, "For God hath set same in the Church, first apostles... secondly prophets...thirdly teachers...next mighty works, among which are the healing of diseases... and *gifts of either speaking or interpreting divers kinds of tongues.* Clearly these are the Church's agents of ministry and work of whom the body of Christ consists; and God has ordained them." (On the Trinity, Vol 8 Chap 33)

- circa 390 AD – Augustine of Hippo, in an exposition on Psalm 32, discusses a phenomenon contemporary to his time of those who "sing in jubilation", singing the praises of God not in their own language, but in a manner that "may not be confined by the limits of syllables" (On Psalm 32, Enarrationes in Psalmos, 32, ii, Sermo 1:8)

If you seek truth, you will find that this gift is alive and well and in practice   both for evangelism and for personal edification.   If speaking in tongues edifies the individual, don't you need more edifying? I know that I need all the edifying that I can get!   Don't rely on the theoretical, dogmatic arguments – like arguing about how many teeth a horse has. Go look around and you'll see that nearly all of the growth in the Church worldwide is in the "charismatic" segment.   The mainline denominations aren't even keeping up with population growth.   Yes, there are excesses and misuses and abuses and counterfeits, but that doesn't mean it's not real – it just means this is a war and the enemy is really good at misdirection and propaganda and misinformation and demoralization of our troops.

If the Holy Spirit can pray FOR you THROUGH you, isn't it just prideful to think that you can pray in English better than the third of the Godhead that lives in you can pray for you? Don't you think maybe you ought to get out of His way and let Him pray however He wants? It's really just that easy. It's not an on/off switch. It's a dial. If you have the Holy Spirit in you, then He's trying to get out somehow. It may be weeping or groaning or singing or some language you don't know. Maybe He'll pray through you in English, but it will be SO pretty and perfect and dead-on that you just know it wasn't really you in control. He's going to find a way to get out, but the less you put Him in a box, the better. If you've got Jesus and you want to pray in tongues, just say you're sorry for telling Him it wasn't real, let Him know you're willing and ask Him to teach you to pray in whatever way He thinks would be the most effective for His Kingdom and bring Him the most glory. It may also help to have someone pray with you.

It's the same with all the gifts. If they are still available, then we NEED them! This is a WAR! It always was! So, if the enemy is a deceiver and liar and a cheat, and anything he has is a cheap counterfeit of what God has – and the enemy has spells and familiar spirits and mediums and psychics and astral projection and zombies – then where is OUR stuff? We used to have people getting healed and seeing angels and prophets and theoportation (moved from one place to another by God) and even people getting raised from the dead! So, if this is a war, how come they got to keep all of their cool toys and we lost our's? That doesn't seem fair. Who would benefit most if giant chunks of our team decided that the war was actually over, the enemy wasn't real and/or we didn't have weapons anymore? I gotta think the bad guys probably made up that bit of propaganda. I can't figure any way that it glorifies God – and it sure looks like we're losing this war!

Anybody that is actually dangerous to satan acknowledges that he is real and is taking him on by the power of the Holy Spirit. Everybody sitting off to the side pretending there is no war, has already been co-opted. Jesus said if you were like Him, all the powers of hell would come gunning for you. He wasn't kidding. If you're comfy, you're probably on the wrong team.

We had someone place curses and ritually sacrifice a cat in front of my furniture store during a prayer meeting! I was thrilled! And to me it was a very real confirmation that something was happening at that little furniture store that discomforted the enemy enough to have some poor, confused kid turn off American Idol, steal the neighbor's cat, drive to the middle of the business district on a Thursday night and ritually sacrifice a cat in front of a furniture store! We got somebody's attention! If nobody is shooting at you, then you're NOT dangerous! How many animals have been sacrificed in front of YOUR "church"? Shouldn't you be a target?

SO WHY SHOULD WE REALLY WANT THE HOLY SPIRIT? DON'T WE ALREADY HAVE THE "FULLNESS" OF THE HOLY SPIRIT IF WE'RE "SAVED"?

Well, I'll leave it to you to decide if you have all the Holy Spirit you can hold – if you're so jammed packed full of Jesus that nothing else can fit and it's just splashing out the top and sprinkling all the people around you. Since I don't think it's a fixed quantity and a one-time thing, I'm not going to be satisfied until I'm transformed by the renewing of my mind, a new creation in Christ, a fearless witness for the Gospel – and my shadow is healing people!

What's the payoff? What was promised to us? Well, here is a list. You decide if you think we are currently getting the full benefits of all of these.

Promises about the Holy Spirit:

- Jesus would come to baptize with the Holy Spirit - and/or with fire (Matt. 3:11; Mark 1:8; Luke 3:16; John 1:33; Acts 1:5; Acts 11:16)

- The Baptism of the Holy Spirit is for all generations (Acts 2:38-39)

- The Baptism of the Holy Spirit will give the necessary power for witnessing (Acts 1:8)

- God gives the Holy Spirit to all those who obey Him (Acts 5:32)

- God confirms the Gospel and our salvation by the gifts of the Holy Spirit (Heb. 2:2-4)

- The Holy Spirit will write God's laws on our heart (Heb. 10:14-17)

- The need for and possibility of regeneration (John 3:6)

- If you are led by the Spirit, you'll be like the wind (John 3:8)

- The promise of the Holy Spirit being given to us all (John 14:17; 15:26; 16:13; Acts 2:17-18)

- If you live according to the Spirit, you are free from condemnation and the flesh (Rom. 8:1, 9; Gal. 5:16-24; Gal. 6:8; Philippians 3:3; I Peter 3:18)

- The Spirit makes us free from the law of sin and death (Romans 8:2)

- If you are led by the Spirit of God, you are the son of God (Romans 8:14)

- When we don't know what to pray, the Spirit will pray for us (Romans 8:26-27)

- The Spirit will wash and sanctify and justify us all (I Corinthians 6:11; Romans 15:16; Titus 3:5)

- The Spirit is the downpayment on our future glory (2 Corinthians 5:5)

- That the Spirit is for all people (Galatians 3:14)

- Much fruit results from following the Spirit (Galatians 5:22-24)

- Will teach us all things and lead us to Truth (John 14:26; 1 Corinithians 2:13)

- Teach us how to wield the Sword which is the Word (Ephesians 6:17)

- When you don't know what to say, He'll give you the words (Mark 13:11; Luke 12:12)

- We can know we are His by the Holy Spirit in us (I John 3:24, 4:13)

- The Spirit will show us Truth because He is Truth (I John 5:6)

- Helps us to keep and guard that good which was committed to us (2 Timothy 1:14)

- The Holy Spirit spreads the love of God abroad through us (Romans 5:5)

- Gives us joy and peace and righteousness and hope (Romans 14:17; Romans 15:13)

- Will confirm the true Gospel when preached (1 Thessalonians 1:5-6; 1 Peter 1:12)

- The Holy Spirit will flow up from inside of you and satisfy your thirst (John 7:37-39)

Wow! That's a lot of stuff! Are you seeing miracles around you confirming your walk with God? Are you full of peace and joy and victory? Have you overcome sin? We're all sinners, but we don't have to stay that way. The Bible says we're a new creation and that the Spirit of God will write His law on our hearts and keep us from sinning!

He justifies and sanctifies and leads us in the paths of righteousness. Is that what your life is like?

Is the Holy Spirit your teacher – or are you listening to Men? Now, certainly, the Holy Spirit can speak through other people, we're one Body and we're supposed to avail ourselves of those people that were given as GIFTS to the Church to teach and preach and gently correct. But ultimately we should only listen to them when JESUS is coming out of their mouth – not self or flesh or man-made stuff. First and foremost, we need to have the kind of relationship with God where He can direct all of our paths and we can hear His voice loud and clear. And for that you need to be walking in holiness and complete commitment to Him. And for <u>that</u> you need the Holy Spirit – there is no way to walk in holiness on your own power!

So how do we do this? Do we have any instructions?

Yes. These listed are just a very few. The main thing is that He doesn't want to share space with all your icky stuff. You have to get washed clean by true repentance to make room and then hunger and thirst for as big a quantity of the Holy Spirit as you can get.

Instructions about the Holy Spirit:

- Be being filled continually (Eph. 5:18)
- Stir up the gift of God in you (2 Tim. 1:6)
- Be good dispensers one into another of the gifts entrusted to you (1 Peter 4:10)

It's not a one-time thing. You need to be filled all the time and in ever-increasing quantity so that you won't be ineffective for the Gospel (I Peter 1). However much you had yesterday, it was JUST enough to get through the trials of that day. If God is going to continue to stretch you, then you're going to need more of Him every day! I can't "muster up" wisdom or long-suffering or brotherly kindness! There is no good thing in me except Jesus! If I need to be more of those things, then He needs to pour it into me because there is no other source for it – and the mechanism by which those things are transferred is by the power of the Holy Spirit.

You need to test the spirits all the time and be sure that you're only getting the good stuff – there are also counterfeits out there! Remember this is a war against the greatest liar in history. Expect him to be sneaky and underhanded and try to use our own assets against us and try to turn our victories into defeats. His favorite thing is getting us to turn on and devour each other. And we're such stupid sheep, we've been playing right into the enemy's hands!

You need to stir up the gift and keep what you have in motion and never bury it in the sand or put a bushel on it or hide it under a bed. And you need to share with each as they have a need, constantly pouring out all that you have and getting a fresh filling. That way the whole of the Body is equipped and lifted up toward maturity. That way we are bonded together and they will know us by our love – by our freakish sacrificial willingness to give of anything that we have, even our BEST stuff which is our treasure in heaven, not just our earthly goods! We're to share with each as they have a need – whatever we have. It really does work.

(More on that in our book "Rain Right NOW, Lord!")

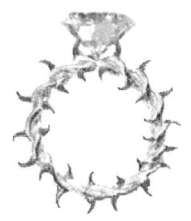

WHAT IF I'M THE ONE THAT IS NEUTERING THE HOLY SPIRIT?!

Oh, dude. That would be really bad! But you totally can, you know. You can put God in a box. If you don't think God can talk to people, then He won't talk to you. If you don't think God heals people, then don't expect anybody in your church to get healed. Just keep praying that the doctors would have wisdom and remember all that they learned in medical school. Send the doctors a nice encouragement letter. Maybe just your "good vibes" will help. That seems like a really sad god to be worshiping if you ask me – but that's the best you can hope for because you've denied the supernatural power of God and quenched the Spirit. So you're on your own power now. Good luck with that. (Luck is pretty much all you've got.)

See, He's very polite. The Holy Spirit is a gentle dove and He won't stay where He's not invited. He doesn't force Himself on people and He will leave the building as soon as you start going your own way and making it about YOU.

There are lots of "churches" where that Gentle Dove hasn't been spotted in YEARS!

The VAST majority of "Christians" in the West have probably never even felt the Holy Spirit move at all. Our structures and systems are so directly and perfectly inverted from the way it is SUPPOSED to work that we just don't leave Him any room at all. And so many of us have adopted doctrines that essentially only leave a little teeny box for the Holy Spirit to occupy – just the "souped-up conscience" box. A gentle nudge to do the right thing. In fact, evidently it's so gentle that it's incapable of keeping 50% of the pastors from using porn and more than half the people in the evangelical churches of America from getting divorced. Never mind sloth, anger, unforgiveness, division, dissension, selfish ambition, envy, lust pride, greed. Hey, wait! Those are the acts of the sinful nature that will keep us from inheriting the kingdom of God! (Galatians 5:19-21). Do you mean that if we're doing that stuff, even if we said the Sinner's Prayer and we're going to church all the time, we might not inherit the kingdom of God? Yep. That's not what I'm saying, that's what the Bible. If you love Him, you'll obey Him. If you don't forgive others, He won't forgive you. If He's not your FIRST priority, then you are worshiping idols. That's bad, right? You probably ought to knock it off.

But how can you? Have you tried rebuking that fear in your own name? Try this, "I rebuke you, vile Spirit of Fear, in the name of Pastor Bob!" See how that works for you. Have you tried to get off of drugs or porn or anger or alcohol in your own power? How did that work for you? Is it all the way gone? Or do you just have to be on guard all the time and constantly fearful that it might pop up at any moment and wreck your life?

Why do you need the Holy Spirit? Because He has the power to completely and totally scrub that stuff out once and for all and make you a new person. I've seen Him do it instantly. Complete and total and instantaneous removal of addictions to drugs and cigarettes and porn and all kinds of stuff. I've seen the Spirit of God do radical transformations on people that result in them being completely unrecognizable to their friends and family. Nobody even knew that it was possible for that cranky, angst-filled teenage girl that was anorexic and "cutting" to actually be happy! But she is – and it won't go away! And it's more than just salvation, it's being FULL – and learning how to stay full all the time. And it's not about "church" - we ARE the church, we don't have to GO to church. It's about being so crammed packed full of Jesus that nothing else can fit. And it's for all of us and it's available today and it will keep you from sin and transform you and make you a new creation and you'll hear God and He will direct all your paths. For real. I'm not making this up. It's all in the Bible. You just have to believe that the Bible means what it says and stop listening to Men.

But it's entirely possible that you're the one that has been neutering the Holy Spirit. In fact, even if you don't have Him in a teeny weeny box, you probably have limited Him somehow. The solution is to say you're sorry (and mean it) and ask Him to bust through all your boxes and just be God to you however He wants. As long as it's Him and you know it's Him and not some counterfeit, just loose Him to relate to you in whatever way HE thinks best. You can be sure that when you ask for bread, he's not going to give you a stone. (Mark 7:9) If you come to Him with a pure heart seeking the real thing, He's not going to allow you to get a counterfeit. He's a good Dad.

41

This is a one-on-one walk we're supposed to be having here. You can't get salvation by proxy through someone else. You can't reliably hear God for yourself if you're taking someone else's word for what God wants you to hear. Regardless of your denomination or theology or anything else, YOU are going to be held responsible for what YOU did with the Gift He gave you. Did you bury it in the sand or did you trade it and invest it wisely and make it grow and bring a great return? (Matthew 25:14-30)

When you stand before God, He is going to ask what YOU did with His Son Jesus (and His Spirit). You won't be able to blame the pastor or the denomination. If you're reading this, you're aware now that you're responsible and that YOU will have to answer for why YOU grieved and blasphemed the Holy Spirit. You can't blame it on John MacArthur or the Bible Answer Man or some heresy hunter website you read. You're a grown up, you can read the Bible, you can seek the Lord, you can answer when He knocks. He's been trying to get through to you, He's been standing at the door and knocking. If you hardened your heart, then the consequences are on your own head.

If this is getting through, maybe you could pray this (or something like it, whatever):

Dear Lord Jesus,

I love You so much. I don't get all of this and I don't get how exactly it might change things, but I know I'm not all the way full. Please, Lord, please, I have to know it's You – I don't want a counterfeit or anything from the enemy and I don't want it to be my own flesh. But I gotta have more of You, Lord!

Please, I'm sorry for whatever I've done to grieve Your Spirit. If there is something in particular that I've done that You want me to repent for specifically, please show it to me and I will, but otherwise, please accept my apology and wash me clean with the Blood of Jesus. I'll try to do better. I didn't know that there was more of You available to me!

Please, Lord, just baptize me or dunk me or marinate me or whatever You have to do so that I'm all the way full, shaken together, packed down and overflowing with the Holy Spirit. Please get any pieces of me out of Your way so that I can walk in the fullness of all that You have for me. I promise to give You all the glory and not make it about me. Please, Abba?

I come to You in faith, believing that this is what You want for me, so I know You're going to answer it. Show me how to reach up and drink from the Fountain of Living Water all the time.

In the Name of Jesus Christ, my Lord. Amen.

YEAH, WHATEVER. HOW BAD COULD IT BE? WHAT CAN THE HOLY SPIRIT DO TO ME ANYWAY?

Oh, you just had to go and ask that, didn't you?! Now we're going to have to get it on! Did you really put the Holy Spirit is such a small box that you think YOU are bigger than HIM?! Oh, that's gonna hurt. I sure hope you hear my warning on this, cause your clock is ticking if you don't. It's bad enough if <u>you</u> believe it, but I sure hope you're not teaching that stuff!

Warnings about the Holy Spirit:

- Blasphemy against the Holy Spirit **will not** be forgiven (Matt. 12:31-32; Mark 3:29; Luke 12:10)

- If you resist Him, you're stiff-necked and uncircumcised in heart (Acts 7:51)

- Don't grieve Him by division in the Body (Eph. 4:30)

- Don't quench the Spirit (1 Thessalonians 5:19)

- Don't insult the Spirit – or else (Hebrews 10:29-30)

- Don't harden your hearts to His voice by your unbelief – or else! (Hebrews 3:7-19)

- The Spirit is jealous and doesn't like you making something else an idol (James 4:5)

- If you try to lie to Him, He might just kill you! (Acts 5:1-10)

- Try/test every spirit to be sure it is of God (I John 4:1-6)

- If you hate, you're not hating man, but God that gave His Spirit (1 Thessalonians 4:8)

- Your Body is the temple of the Holy Spirit, not your own (I Corinithians 6:19)

- Those without the Spirit will persecute you (Gal. 4:29; Gal. 5:17)

- It's **impossible** for those who were once enlightened and have tasted the heavenly gift and were made partakers in the Holy Spirit and the Word of God and the power of the world to come, and then fall away, to be renewed again unto repentance (Hebrews 6:4-5)

I think He sort of mentioned this stuff in the Old Testament warnings, too. What is "blasphemy against the Holy Spirit"? Well, in the context of that passage, people were saying that Jesus was delivering demons, but even though the Holy Spirit was doing it, they were giving satan credit for it. So they were denying that the Holy Spirit was real or there or powerful or at work and instead glorified the enemy, who was the one getting exorcised!

Again, if you start telling folks that God doesn't heal people and that every faith healer on TV is full of satan and it's satan healing people, then; A) you have to show me where in the Bible satan heals anybody, B) you have explain how a house divided can stand, C) you have to understand that if EVEN ONE person actually did get healed by the power of the Holy Spirit, but you are so careless with your words as to give the enemy ALL the credit, then you've blasphemed the Holy Spirit. If anyone is speaking in Tongues and it IS real and for today and for spreading the Gospel and IS being used Biblically and appropriately, but you insist that ALL tongues are of the devil, then you've blasphemed the Holy Spirit. Are you getting this? And I don't know exactly what the requirements or limitations of this threat are, but JESUS Himself said that people that do that WILL NEVER be forgiven for it. You might want to be extra, EXTRA careful.

And one of the very best ways to grieve the Holy Spirit is by encouraging, sanctioning, tolerating, aiding, participating in division in the Body of Christ. We're not just talking about the local congregation, we're talking about the whole Body. We have 41,000+ denominations now, how could He not be stomping mad furious with us?! How could the Holy Spirit not be grieved by this horrible mess we've made? And we told them it was God that told us to do it!

Listen, buddy, let me warn you. You don't know who you're messing with here. This is a third of the Godhead you're poking at. He'll send a strong delusion on you destined for your destruction and you won't even know He did it (that's what "strong delusion" means). You'll be sure you're hearing God, even while the ATF and FBI are rolling tanks into your living room. You'll be absolutely positive that you are God's chosen messenger and that you're hearing Him and testing the spirits and know what you're doing, all the way to the bottom of the cooler of poisoned Kool-aid.

You'll have a worldwide TV ministry and be building an amusement park and have air conditioners in your dog houses and the next thing you know, you'll be in jail for something. You might even be the president of the National Association of Evangelicals and have the President of the United States on your speed dial, but before you know it you're having sex with your gay masseuse and exposed on the same Fox News channel that used to love you. And you'll never even know what hit you until it's too late.

DO NOT underestimate God! Go read Deuteronomy 28. If you disobey He will crush you like a bug. And it even says, "Just as it pleased me to see you prosper, it will please me to destroy you." (Deuteronomy 28:63) If you go your own way, He will see to it that you end up eating your own children. WOW! We're not teaching THAT in Sunday School! This is a jealous God we're talking about here. Yes, He's a warm, fuzzy, loving shepherd. But He's more than that, too. "It is a fearful thing to fall into the hands of a living God." (Hebrews 10:31) Do you know why shepherds carry little lambs around their necks? Because when a little lamb won't behave and keeps running off, the shepherd dislocates or breaks their leg, then sets it and carries them until it heals. THEN that little lamb will be so bonded and dependent on the shepherd that it will NEVER run away again. He does it out of love and knowing what is best for the lamb. You know all those pictures of Jesus as the loving shepherd with a little lamb around His neck ... it's because He broke it's leg! I know He's done it to me and He's probably done it to you. And I'd like Him not to have to do it to me any more than necessary!

He might hit you with a bus, but He might also just lift His hand the tiniest little bit and let you go your own way. He might just give you the desires of your heart, which has something to do with your secretary's cleavage. And it will wreck your life. He might even send more and more people to your congregation so that it would grow and you'd be famous and feel like God is blessing you and money is rolling in and you get a new book deal – and you are getting farther and farther from the broken, contrite vessel that is actually useful to God. Before you know it, that radical, Jesus freak, idealistic first-time pastor is a Purpose-driven, big-church institutional sell-out with a new gym and a chandelier in the sanctuary – and a congregation full of bleeding, sucking spiritual chest wounds with no help on the horizon. And you'll just be as happy as a clam while you lead them all down the broad way straight to hell.

If you go your own way, if you get out from under His headship, then anything that wants to will shoot at you – and He will let it have at you until you repent, but you can't repent when you're under a strong delusion that convinces you that you're just fine. But the only solution is to repent – but you can't. Get it? You're in a "Catch 22" until He thinks you've had enough and have learned your lesson. Read this - www.FellowshipOfTheMartyrs.com/red_dragon.htm .

I've seen it. I've felt it. I know about the wrath of God and the love of God. NONE of us can get our head around the extremes of either one – and yet He is both. You can't leave one out and say that you have a complete understanding of God.

Want some Biblical examples?

People who HAD the Holy Spirit and then were filled with something else later:

- King Saul – filled with an evil spirit FROM GOD! (I Samuel 16:14)

- Ananias and Sapphira – and dropped dead! (Acts 5:1-10)

- Deceived Christians (I Timothy 4:1) - *"Now the Spirit speaketh expressly, that in the latter times some shall depart from the faith, giving heed to seducing spirits, and doctrines of devils;"*

What kinds of doctrines of devils? Oh, maybe that devils aren't real and that we don't need to fight them and we don't actually have any weapons anymore. That sounds like a doctrine a devil would like you to buy into, doesn't it? Or that if we say so many "Hail Mary's" and "Our Fathers" we can keep on drinking and cussing and playing the field and being not at all like Jesus the rest of the week and we're just fine. Or maybe that God wants all Christians to be rich and fat and comfy. Or maybe that God loves America so much that He'll rapture us out before any shooting starts so we won't have to actually endure any persecution (even though Christians pretty much everywhere else already are!).

Oh! Or the big one, that if we just say this little "Sinner's Prayer" then we can pretty much do whatever we want after that and we're perfectly safe and can be sure that we're going to heaven no matter what. Never mind Lordship or obedience or self-sacrifice. Never mind being crucified daily or being perfect as He is perfect – just "repeat after me." How can that be the "Narrow Way"?! Salvation is just a mantra said once? Like Ali Baba opening a magic door if he just says the right phrase? Sure seems like a Broad Road to me. (Matt. 7:13)

I'm just REAL sure that that was a doctrine of devils, because it sure ain't in the Bible and it has caused MILLIONS, maybe hundreds of millions, to miss the whole point. The New Testament would be a lot shorter if it all boiled down to "Accept Jesus into your heart, say this prayer and you'll be saved." In fact, there is no such thing like that anywhere in the Bible. We're to work out our salvation with fear and trembling. We're to walk humbly before our God as broken and contrite vessels useful for His purposes. We're to surrender ALL!

If we just need to accept Jesus as our "Savior", then how come the Bible refers to Him that way so few times?

618 times as Lord	32 times as Lamb
543 times as Christ	**15 times as Savior**
84 times as Son of Man	15 times as Prophet
42 times as Teacher	11 times as Master
37 times as Son of God	7 times as High Priest
35 times as King	

Source: "A Saving Faith" by Bernie Koerselman, Berean Publishers, page 24. E-book available free online at http://www.bereanpublishers.com .

How much do you need to obey the lifeguard that pulled you out of the ocean when you were drowning? Maybe you send him a Christmas card for a few years. Maybe you think fondly of him and are grateful for him having saved you, but you don't obey him daily and let him direct all your paths! But "LORD," "Messiah," or "Christ" is a different thing altogether. If He is your Master and you are His servant then you don't get to direct your own paths. He's a King! You should bow in His presence, wait on His every word and do whatever He tells you.

I'm warning you. Don't toy with the Godhead. Don't go saying He's powerless and He changes. I don't want to hear your talk about some "Dispensation" where God stopped being who He was before. Yes, He changes the way He relates to us as we mature, individually and collectively, but He doesn't change who He is and He doesn't stop doing supernatural things. He's GOD. He's NOT "natural". He can't help but be supernatural. And when He touches stuff supernatural things happen. That's by definition.

If there is a dispensation where the Holy Spirit is powerless, then what else is variable? How else might God change without warning us ahead of time? And how come the enemy isn't powerless?

If anything, as we mature and are more able to handle responsibility and walk in love and submission and brokenness, He would be pouring out MORE of His Spirit and the miracle working power that goes along with it. When we actually grow up into Him who is the Head, maybe we can be trusted with the fullness of the really cool toys. (Ephesians 4:15) If we're not seeing the kind of signs and wonders that were seen by the first Apostles (and are happening around the world as we speak), then maybe it's because the Christians in America are barely able to digest the milk they're being fed and can't handle solid meat.

I Corinthians 3:1-4 (KJV)

1 And I, brethren, could not speak unto you as unto spiritual, but as unto carnal, even as unto babes in Christ. 2 I have fed you with milk, and not with meat: for hitherto ye were not able to bear it, neither yet now are ye able. 3 For ye are yet carnal: for whereas there is among you envying, and strife, and divisions, are ye not carnal, and walk as men? 4 For while one saith, I am of Paul; and another, I am of Apollos; are ye not carnal?

Just so we're more clear and nobody can blame a misunderstanding on King James' olde English.

1 Corinthians 3:1-4 (God's Word version)
1 Brothers and sisters, I couldn't talk to you as spiritual people but as people still influenced by your corrupt nature. You were infants in your faith in Christ. 2 I gave you milk to drink. I didn't give you solid food because you weren't ready for it. Even now you aren't ready for it 3 because you're still influenced by your corrupt nature. When you are jealous and quarrel among yourselves, aren't you influenced by your corrupt nature and living by human standards? 4 When some of you say, "I follow Paul" and others say, "I follow Apollos," aren't you acting like {sinful} humans?

I bet that's like; "I'm for Luther," or "I'm for Calvin," or "I follow Menno," or "I'm for Mike Bickle," or "I follow Paige Patterson," or "I follow T.D. Jakes." I bet that's why we're still being bottle-fed and seem to be losing ground daily to radical, Jesus-loving freaks like the Church in China. If we were mature, we'd be following JESUS CHRIST and making HIM our head instead of some MAN! We'd hear His voice and OBEY all the time. We'd be HIS sheep and not need hired shepherds – who, by the way, are in for a rude awakening when the True Shepherd shows up and appoints His own Under-Shepherds instead of the ones we voted into office to tickle our ears! You might want to read Ezekiel 34. (And weep, repent and mourn before it's too late.)

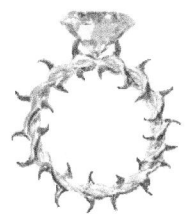

IF MORE HOLY SPIRIT IS AVAILABLE TO ME, HOW DO I GET IT?

Good question. This is kind of important, isn't it? If there's more out there, I want it and I need to know how to get it!

Transferal of the Holy Spirit (or Gifts or Healing) by the laying on of hands:

- Moses to Joshua (Deuteronomy 34:9)

- Peter and John to the Samaritan believers who were saved, but hadn't received the Spirit yet (Acts 8:15-20)

- Ananias to Saul (Acts 9:17)

- Paul to the believers in Ephesus (Acts 19:6)

- Paul heals by laying on hands (Acts 28:8)

- Elders to Timothy (1 Timothy 4:14)

- Paul to Timothy (2 Timothy 1:6)

- Presumably Paul to the Romans if he could get there (Romans 1:11)

- Great Commission charges all believers to lay hands on the sick (Mark 16:18)

This is the most common way seen in the Bible and, in actual practice, the most common way it's done in the churches that practice this still today. There is something about coming together in person and actual physical contact that is really powerful.

The Bible also cautions this:

> **1 Tim 5:22** - *Lay hands suddenly on no man, neither be partaker of other men's sins: keep thyself pure.*

Some "chunks" of the Church (that don't believe the Holy Spirit moves like this) interpret verse that to mean that laying on of hands is only for commissioning services to send out missionaries or ordain someone – and that they are not to do that without extensive personality testing and ordination committee meetings and group votes on the acceptability of the candidates doctrine and adherence to denominational policies. Sadly man-like isn't it?

But I think it means what it says, "Don't lay hands suddenly on anybody, lest you be partaker of their sins." It's a dangerous thing to have people "pour" stuff into you. There are all kinds of ways that the enemy can sneak in. Whether it's something of the enemy or just "soul force" and self, it's REALLY important to make sure that you're fully armored up and covered in the Blood of Jesus before you lay hands on anybody. You don't want to give them something that they aren't ready for, or some piece of your own "self" that they shouldn't have and you don't want to receive anything from them that isn't what God wants for you. More on that later, but the point is that God will not give you a stone if you ask for bread. He is a good Father. So when someone lays hands on you, DO NOT make THEM an idol and seek whatever they have! DO NOT ask the Lord to make you like them. Ask the Lord to give you ONLY whatever He wants for you. All good gifts come from the Father. If you go with a pure heart, covered in the Blood and seeking Jesus – you'll get Jesus. If you go seeking a manifestation, or a gift so your ministry will be famous, you'll be rolling on the floor, clucking like a chicken before you know it. If your motivation is lust, He'll turn you over to the enemy! Don't partake in their sins.

Receiving of the Holy Spirit by just hearing the Truth of the Gospel preached:

- Gentiles in the house of Cornelius (Acts 10)

Sometimes all we need to do is be in a situation where the Holy Spirit is speaking through someone (as He was when Peter was testifying of the Truth of the Gospel). That creates a "bubble" in which the Holy Spirit can move freely because we're not going about our own agenda, but glorifying the Son and speaking to the immediate needs of the people. Sometimes all someone needs is to see the possibility, and their eyes are opened, their heart is hungry and the Lord swoops in and satisfies their heart. This is altogether TOO rare in the "church" today. Mostly we're obsessed with our own agendas. The true Gospel, a call for repentance and absolute submission to the King, is very, very rare.

Please note, they were not in a "church" – this was a private home. And there was no special music or liturgical responsive reading or offering or announcements or anything! They didn't have to go through eight weeks of the "Purpose Driven Life" before they could be "members". They just believed in faith and received. And nobody could deny that they needed to be baptized in water right on the spot. Because they were desperately hungry for God, were shown that He is real and can satisfy their hunger, they sought Him and found Him.

Receiving of the Holy Spirit (or a Gift) by "sucking" it out:

- The woman with a blood disease drawing power from Jesus garment (Mark 5:24-34, Matt. 9:19-22)

- People believing in faith that they could draw power from Peter's shadow (Acts 5:15)

- Jairus knew that if Jesus would just touch his daughter, she'd be healed (Mark 5:23)

- Handkerchiefs that had touched Paul's skin were healing people (Acts 19:12)

You can get your cup full alone in a closet. You can get your cup full with the help of others. You can get your cup full when the Lord speaks to you about His majesty in a sunset or a starry sky or the Rocky Mountains. He is all around. He is right beside you. Reach out and touch the hem of His garment and ask Him for whatever you need. If you seek Him, you will find Him. Just stop telling Him what He can and can't do.

Receiving the Holy Spirit by "drinking" it in:

- David's thirst (Psalm 42; Psalm 63:1-6; Psalm 143:6-12)

- The Lord's instruction through Isaiah (Isaiah 55:1-2) *"1 Ho, every one that thirsteth, **come ye to the*** *waters, and he that hath no money; come ye, buy, and eat; yea, come, buy wine and milk without money and without price. 2 Wherefore do ye spend money for that which is not bread? and your labour for that which satisfieth not? hearken diligently unto me, and eat ye that which is good, and let your soul delight itself in fatness."*

- The instruction of Paul – (I Corinthians 12:13) *"13 For by one Spirit are we all baptized into one body, whether we be Jews or Gentiles, whether we be bond or free; and **have been all made to drink into one Spirit.**"*

- Jesus' own Sermon on the Mount (Matthew 5:3-12) *3 Blessed are the poor in spirit: for theirs is the kingdom of heaven. 4 Blessed are they that mourn: for they shall be comforted. 5 Blessed are the meek: for they shall inherit the earth. 6 **Blessed are they which do hunger and thirst after righteousness: for they shall be filled.** 7 Blessed are the merciful: for they shall obtain mercy. 8 Blessed are the pure in heart: for they shall see God. 9 Blessed are the peacemakers: for they shall be called the children of God. 10 Blessed are they which are persecuted for righteousness' sake: for theirs is the kingdom of heaven. 11 Blessed are ye, when men shall revile you, and persecute you, and shall say all manner of evil against you falsely, for my sake. 12 Rejoice, and be exceeding glad: for great is your reward in heaven: for so persecuted they the prophets which were before you.*

- Jesus and the Woman at the Well (John 4:10) *10 Jesus answered and said unto her, If thou* *knewest the gift of God, and who it is that saith to thee, Give me to drink; thou wouldest have asked of him, and he would have given thee living water. 11 The woman saith unto him, Sir, thou hast nothing to draw with, and the well is deep: from whence then hast thou that living water? 12 Art thou greater than our father Jacob, which gave us the well, and drank thereof himself, and his children, and his cattle? 13 Jesus answered and said unto her, Whosoever drinketh of this water shall thirst again: 14 **But whosoever drinketh of the water that I shall give him shall never thirst; but the water that I shall give him shall be in him a well of water springing up into everlasting life.***

- The promise of Jesus - (John 7:37-39) *"37 In the last day, that great day of the feast, Jesus stood and cried, saying, If any man thirst, let him come unto me, and drink. 38 He that believeth on me, as the scripture hath said, **out of his belly shall flow rivers of living water.** 39 (**But this spake he of the Spirit**, which they that believe on him should receive: for the Holy Ghost was not yet given; because that Jesus was not yet glorified.)"*

Did you get all that? The Bible says that fountains or rivers or streams or wells of LIVING Water will flow up from INSIDE of us! That is our birthright! Do you feel that happening to you? Do you know how to stick a straw in the River of Life and suck until you're full? Maybe your "cup" is all full of the wrong kind of stuff and there's no room. Maybe you put a cork on it by unforgiveness or fear or bitterness. Maybe you have your hand over the top of your cup because you think you've had enough – or already gotten all that was available.

This river – this water – that we're talking about is the Holy Spirit. He is the "fluid" that fills our cup. He is that which is the righteousness of God that writes the Law of the Lord on our hearts. We are to be FULL and to keep getting full – otherwise the enemy has room to jump in and mess with us. AND we are to crucify pieces of ourselves daily, so that He can increase and we can decrease. More on that later.

You should be able to see from these verses what we're supposed to be doing, but this is what we've actually done.

> ***Jer 2:11-13*** - *11 Hath a nation changed their gods, which are yet no gods? but my people have changed their glory for that which doth not profit. 12 Be astonished, O ye heavens, at this, and be horribly afraid, be ye very desolate, saith the LORD. 13 For my people have committed two evils; they have forsaken me the fountain of living waters, and hewed them out cisterns, broken cisterns, that can hold no water.*

They hewed out their own cisterns? Do you know what that is? A cistern is a large container to hold lots of water. Typically it would be a big vat in the ground used to hold water for a whole group or tribe to drink from when there was a need. The Children of God dug these artificial vats and tried to store up their own water – but they leak! They should have just trusted God   the fountain of living water – and believed that He would supply their need as they needed it, but instead, they tried to store it up. Like the manna in the desert that only lasted for one day, if they tried to store it, it would go bad. They had to trust in God's daily provision and not trust in the work of their own hands.

They built large vats to store the water, but it doesn't work, their cisterns are leaking. AND they have irritated God by not leaning on Him and trusting Him for their provision!

Do you know what the spiritual equivalent to those cisterns is today? It's the institutional churches that are building large containers (buildings, sanctuaries, storehouses, barns) and convincing people that they are the place to come to get the Living Water. But they are leaking and can't contain it – or are lukewarm and stagnant and stale trying to recycle old water (or never had any in there in the first place). They are full of day-old manna that doesn't satisfy – and in fact, it is poisoning the people, who are pretending that it tastes good because everyone else around them is pretending that it tastes good!

The living water flows up from INSIDE of us. We ARE the Church. We don't need large communal cisterns where someone has stored up old, stale water. We need the fountains to flow from our own bellies! We need to learn how to reach out and touch the hem of Jesus' garment and suck. We need to stick a straw in the river that flows from the Throne of God and drink until we're full – and then learn how to stay full all the time! It really does work like that. It's just that it requires faith like a child and laying down all our artificial devices and seeing the complete uselessness of the leaky cisterns that we've built on our own power when we turned away and forsook the Fountain of Living Water. Only when we are personally full can we then go and truly BE the Church to a lost and dying world.

We need to get unclogged and get the fountains that are supposed to be flowing up from our own bellies moving again!

God forgive us. We made this way too hard. All we ever had to do was teach them to get their cup all cleaned out, keep it cleaned out, reach up and hold Jesus' hand and suck really hard. But we tried to satisfy their God-given spiritual thirst with our own devices and programs and entertainments. And they're dying all around us and the enemy is eating them for lunch – and we're pretending everything is just fine.

Who benefits most from a theology that says the River dried up or that you get one shot glass full and that's all you're ever going to get? What a sad walk with God that would be? I need Him in INCREASING quantity daily so that I won't be ineffective and unproductive for the Gospel (2 Peter 1:2-11)

So who benefits most from a fixed-quantity, one-time only, Holy Spirit theology? Yep. Gotta be the bad guys. Cause the Bible says that it will overflow out of us and be endless.

Horse Teeth Reality Check

I know people that have had folks lay hands on them and impart (share) with them supernaturally and instantly the gift of fluently playing the piano or drums or other things.

I personally had a Gift of Administration shared with me by a brother in Houston. It started to express itself immediately and I've shared it with others as the Lord has directed. In my old business, I would work at a desk until the piles of stuff overwhelmed it, then we would rope it off and I'd move to another desk! Now I'm keeping better records, my van is cleaned out, I'm

---

making the bed, I'm aware of small details, and I'm doing other stuff that I used to think was creepy – but I really needed these skills for what God is calling me to do.

A sister, that used to be on crack and all kinds of bad, dark things before the Lord rescued her and lit her up, was sent to my furniture store. She had been so deep into enemy territory that she is hypersensitive to the bad guys. She pretty much sees demons on people all the time – and can tell you exactly what is messing with them. If there is a war, I want to SEE the bad guys, not just blast away in the dark hoping I hit something. I had sought the Lord and the Gift of Discernment of Spirits. This sister and many others came and shared with me of the wealth of their inheritance. Over the last two years, like a new wine, all these different, special grapes have blended together and helped me to see better and better in the spirit. As the Lord allows, now I pretty much see whatever is messing with someone and can tell them what it is, where it came from, how long it's been there, what it's saying and what we need to do to get it off and keep the doors closed. The fruit from that has been amazing as LOTS of people have had the chains broken and the yokes lifted.

A brother in Kansas City that I know sings in the Spirit, a verse in tongues and the interpretation in English – original prophetic compositions that can sometimes go on for hours. The Lord said I should ask him to share that with me. He did and three days later I started getting and writing down new songs.

When the Lord first gave me a linguistic tongue to pray with it was a complete language package that I could translate on the fly. I can read the Bible in it, I can conjugate verbs – it is a language of Man, some kind of Native American that we haven't identified yet. Since then, He has given me other tongues for warfare, for messages to the Church, for intercession, for communication and other things. All of them edify me in some way. Praise God! I need all the edifying I can get!

I have shared with others or had shared with me; peace, discernment of spirits, wisdom, faith, boldness, knowledge, languages, self-control, interpretation of tongues and more. I have seen the fruits of that over and over and over as they manifest and equip people to walk closer to the Lord or to be better leaders or elders. It is absolutely imperative that we "share with each as they have a need" – clearly that instruction includes a bag of groceries or some warm clothes – but our spiritual assets are much more valuable and just as transferable. God's economy says that if I give something away sacrificially, He will give me more! We're not waiting on Him to pour out His Spirit on all flesh, He is waiting on us to stop being lukewarm and stagnant and sharing with each all that He has already given us! And then the endless rivers of living water can flow!

We're known by the word of our testimony. I don't expect you to believe it, but this is my testimony. It's true because I've seen it and felt it and know it to be true. Disbelieve me if you like, but you CANNOT convince me that what I saw with my own eyes didn't happen because it disagrees with your theology. I've just seen too many miracles for me to buy that line anymore.

Read this for more:

www.FellowshipOfTheMartyrs.com/rain_right_now.htm

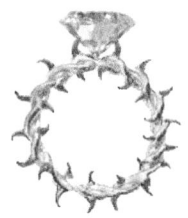

HAVE APOSTLES AND PROPHETS CEASED TOO?

What the Cessationists seem to miss, and most others who are intent on their one, single interpretation and application of the Bible being the right and only one, is that the Bible is spiral. There are multiple applications. They argue not only that certain gifts have ceased, but also that certain offices and callings have ceased. That God gave certain people as "gifts" to the Church at one point – but evidently he doesn't give us those gifts anymore.

The most common argument is that of Ephesians 2:20. That the Church was built on the foundation of the Apostles and Prophets and that foundation is laid and final and therefore those offices have ceased.

Eph 2:19-22 (ASV)

19 So then ye are no more strangers and sojourners, but ye are fellow-citizens with the saints, and of the household of God, 20 being built upon the foundation of the apostles and prophets, Christ Jesus himself being the chief corner stone; 21 in whom each several building, fitly framed together, groweth into a holy temple in the Lord; 22 in whom ye also are builded together for a habitation of God in the Spirit.

My problem with that is two fold. First, is the "horse teeth" reality check that I happen to have met true apostles and prophets that meet all the Biblical criteria for such. Second, that argument is entirely focused on the MACRO application and ignores all the other possible spirals.

For example, can Jesus Christ be the chief cornerstone in my life? Yes. In my congregation? Yes. In the Body of Christ in my city? Yes. In the Universal Church? Yes. Can He be all of those things at the same time? Yes. He is very versatile. But we are human and it may require multiple people to fulfill all those roles on each of the different "legs" of the spiral.

So which "church" is it that we are building upon the foundation of the apostles and prophets? All of them. Does the Universal Church need a foundation laid other than that laid by the Apostles and Prophets of the First Church? No. But is the role of the apostle as one that is sent to plant and to nurture and to serve still valid today? Yes. Is there still a need for the prophet that speaks the application of the Bible to the sinfulness of a society and calls for their repentance? Yes. Are there people whom God has called and touched who have done that throughout history? Yes. Does it require fresh, extra-Biblical revelation in order to be a prophet or apostle? No, not necessarily. Should they have authority to add to the canon (the Bible)? No. Can the Lord help them to see something that is in the Bible, but their contemporaries have missed and need to hear? Yes. How would He tell them that? By revelation from the Holy Spirit.

Prophecy is still for today because the Bible says that the testimony of Jesus IS the spirit of prophecy. (Rev. 19:10) Unless Jesus has ceased or His testimony has ceased, then when we reveal to people His nature and tell His story, we are prophesying. This may be reading the Bible to them or it may be showing them the application of it to their own lives. Or it may be speaking a personal word to them that He wants them to hear about how He wants to be involved in their lives. Whatever it is, it will line up with Scripture if it's from Him.

Said another way, my argument is that the only Biblical model for the local church is the City Church. One autonomous body per town. I can find no other model. I can find no Biblical justification for denominations or hierarchical structures that exceed one town in size. I can find absolutely no justification for a popish Roman model that elevates one man to be God's mouthpiece and have autocratic authority to direct the affairs of many. The Church of Jerusalem allows for no further division within it. They are to be one body within each locality and they are to be entirely independent of Laodicea or Ephesus or Smyrna or Antioch or any other. They are sisters, but none can lord it over another. There is no "Bishop of Asia Minor" – the letters in Revelation are to each independent "ekklesia" or local body of "those who are called out".

And in each town, the Lord sent apostles and prophets, not just to lay down the original foundation, but also to serve and to correct and to impart and to teach and to give personal words of prophecy that didn't have canonical implications but were CRITICALLY important to a particular individual. (Acts 21:11) Paul was sent back to places he had previously been, not to lay a foundation other than what he had already laid, but to make corrections or to strengthen or to encourage. Did God send Apostles to places to do things OTHER THAN re-lay a foundation? Yes. Did God send Apostles sometimes to show people that they had accepted another Jesus and were building incorrectly? Yes. Why isn't that still needed today? Are our Bodies all on the right foundations? Are any of us preaching another Jesus?

There were Apostles with a capital "A". There were only a handful (12+Paul) and they had a specific purpose and season. They sit around the throne of God and are special for a host of reasons, including their suffering for His sake. They are gone from the earth. But that doesn't mean that the office necessarily stopped. There were lower case "a" apostles acknowledged in the Bible – like Luke and John Mark and Barnabas and Junia – more than twenty of them. And today there are still lower case "a" apostles who serve and suffer and plant and minister and weep and are known by their having seen Jesus, by their obedience, by their crucifying of their flesh, by their love, and by their freakishly high gifts of faith.

Said another way, if the purpose of the Prophets was to establish the canon (Bible) and the foundation of the Church, but there were prophets at the time that were clearly prophets but don't seem to have had any impact or application canonically, then what were they doing there? Agabus and Philip's daughters and Ananias and many others seem to have played entirely peripheral and local roles and had no canonical significance. If they were around then, why can't they be around now? If the only purpose of apostles and prophets was to lay the foundation for THE Universal Church, than how do we explain those that the Bible recognizes as apostles and prophets but didn't have a global impact?

And if they were only there to establish the Church, then what are they doing in the Old Testament? If the Holy Spirit was doing THEN the same stuff He did AFTER Pentecost, then why exactly do we think it needed to stop? And which apostles and prophets exactly was it that laid the foundation for the Church? Daniel, David, Moses, Peter, Paul? Yes. And others that never got their names in there at all, but played pivotal roles in historically setting the stage or plowing the ground.

My argument is that the City Church is the thing and that each one requires being set on the proper foundation and being established so that it can be built up. The true apostles and prophets of today establish the same foundation as did the Apostles – Christ and Him crucified. They build on right doctrine and they build on love. They establish the local Body through harmony and prayer and patient long-suffering and much affliction. They use their mighty weapons of war to pull down principalities and powers and spiritual wickedness in high places. They do not lead forcibly, they are not autocrats, they do not enforce anything – they are gifts to the churches and they serve and show by their lives how it's to be done. And signs and wonders confirm them to the degree that the Lord wills. The best signs and wonders are radically transformed lives of freedom and peace and joy, not the ability to predict an earthquake or a drought.

You can read more on that here:
www.FellowshipOfTheMartyrs.com

You can read more about the roles of apostles in the first four chapters here:
http://www.fellowshipofthemartyrs.com/pdf/normal%20christian%20church_all.pdf

Final Horse Teeth Reality Check

Do people get raised from the dead today? You decide.
http://www.shepherdserve.org/special_reports/daniel_main.htm

Does God do miracles in America? Can God move through kids at a football game? What is God doing in Haiti?http://KingdomPowerOnTheStreet.blogspot.com

Muslims all over the world are having dreams and visions of Jesus. http://isaalmasih.net/isa/dreamsofisa.html

One of many encounters with God documented here: http://www.jesus.org.uk/ja/mag_sp2007_dream.shtml

My personal experience includes 4 1/2 months in a van driving 17,500+ miles to 32 states entirely dependent on God for every direction, dollar, and appointment. He was always faithful and daily miracles resulted, not only of divine appointments all over the country, but also physical healings, deliverance of oppressions of all kinds, impartation of gifts to me and thru me, spiritual warfare of all kinds, and even playful fun time with the Lord when He met some of my wants, not just my needs. That story and other radical testimonies are here: fellowshipofthemartyrs.com/home/index.php/testimonies/dougs-testimony.html One of the stops on my trip was here- fellowshipofthemartyrs.com/manchester.htm

Read the **"The Heavenly Man"** by Hattaway and Yun. This book will mess you up! Brother Yun fasted 73 days in a Chinese prison without food or water, tortured, beaten, broken. AND miraculously healed, broken out of prison, given Bibles by Communist prison officials, angelic protection, escaped from the country and more. This kind of stuff is common in the persecuted church. (However, it is rare in the comfy, fat, lazy, rich church.)

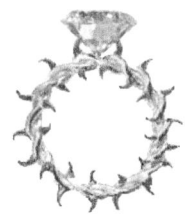

THIRTEEN EASY WAYS TO GRIEVE THE HOLY SPIRIT

- Tell Him when to show up and when to leave. Schedule His appearances and make sure everyone knows that <u>you</u> have control of His reins so that He will be gone in time for everyone to get to Sunday lunch on time.

- Let somebody that isn't anointed and isn't supposed to be speaking run the show.

- Tell God how great He is and how much you love and adore Him and sing songs to Him while you completely ignore all the bleeding people around you. Tell them to call the office if they want to talk to someone, but don't disrupt the carefully planned presentation that was scheduled for this time period.

- Divide the Body of Christ up into smaller and smaller pieces and fill it with dissension, factions, division, selfish ambition, strife, quarreling, etc. That's a sure fire way to get the Gentle Dove to take off.

- Tell Him what He can and can't do. Be absolutely positive that you know how He operates and make sure and tell everyone that you have all the answers. Then program and plan and schedule everything in your own power and don't leave Him any room (or any invitation) to show up.

- Give lip service to wanting Him to show up, but don't really mean it or get out of His way. If He does actually try to break through, squelch it as fast as you can. Pray fervently that the Lord would "shake things up" - but when He does, deny it was Him and go back to sleep.

- Cancel your prayer meetings because people are on their faces crying out to the Lord and it's "creepy". We need people to be HAPPY in church! It's just not "en vogue" to have people crying all the time.

- Convince the people that worshiping the Holy Spirit and getting HIM to come is the goal. Seek manifestations and displays of emotionality above all else. (We DO want Him to show up – but as a confirming side effect of fact that the Truth is being spoken and the Gospel is being spread and people are being transformed – not as the whole point of the meeting so that we can just all lay around and giggle.)

- Tell people that something glorious that He did wasn't actually Him.

- Take all of the spiritual assets that the Lord has given you and hoard them and don't share with anybody – and make sure you let everyone know that you are special.

- Make sure that <u>only</u> people with the proper degrees and certifications from approved structures and systems of men are allowed to speak. Whatever you do, <u>don't</u> let the person there that has the biggest cup of Jesus say anything!

- Lie to the people in your congregation about spiritual gifts. Maybe even publicly deny that YOU speak in tongues – when you actually do. That will make Him leave for sure.

- Make it all about <u>YOU</u>. Your Kingdom, Your Power, Your Glory, Forever. Amen.

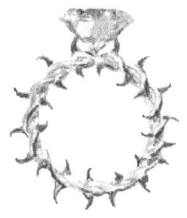

WHAT DO I DO NOW?

If you've been grieving Him, knock it off and say you're sorry. Ask Him to show you how to keep from doing it anymore. Wait on the Lord – don't try to fill all the dead air with YOU.

If you need more Holy Spirit than you've got, read Appendix A and it will walk you through more about how to get unclogged and get your cup full and keep it full all the time.

If you read this whole thing and never disagreed with me on anything, you were probably on board all along and I'm just preaching to the choir and you should have probably put it down and gone out and told someone about Jesus during this whole time you've been reading something that you already knew. Are you sure God told you to read this? (Just checking.)

If you are really, REALLY hungry for more Jesus and you don't care what it takes to get more and you're willing to have Him kill all the parts of you that are in His way, you might consider praying something like this:

(But I warn you in the strongest possible terms, He <u>WILL</u> take you seriously and it <u>WILL</u> hurt.)

Dear Lord,

I trust You. I know You won't push it too far. I know You'll get me through anything. I'm sorry for all the ways I've limited You and failed to obey Your instructions. I'm sorry for having grieved the Holy Spirit over and over by going my own way. I know there is a lot of blood on my head. Please forgive me and wash me clean.

And so that I don't do anything like this ever again, please do whatever You have to do to me so that I'll be so jammed, packed full of Jesus that nothing else can fit. Anything in me that is resisting You in any way, please shred it, kill it, rip it, burn it – if I don't know how to lay it down, then tear it out of my grip. Just do whatever You have to do. I don't care what it costs, I don't care how much it hurts, just crucify all the pieces of me that are in Your way.

And I know You may have to turn up the refining fire pretty high to get me finished cooking, so I'm asking You to just ignore me completely when I bang on the door of the oven and ask You to turn it down. Dial it all the way up and get this turkey done!

Please, Abba. I mean it. There's a war and I want to be fully ready. Get me out of Boot Camp. Do whatever You have to do and get me ready for war. I want to see the bad guys and I want to have the spiritual authority to crush them. I need wisdom and I need more of Your

Spirit and Your love. I want You to get all the glory. It's Your kingdom, Your power, Your glory – forever.

Please, Lord, do whatever you have to do with me. You can have all my stuff, all my dreams, all my relationships. I put it ALL on the altar. Have Your way, Lord. I know this prayer is inside Your will, so I know You're going to answer it. Just don't let go of my hand when it hurts. Please, Father.

In the Name of Jesus Christ my Lord. Amen.

If we can help you, let us know. If you're supposed to help us, let us know. We love you and we're not going to stop loving you no matter what.

Email us at: fotm@fellowshipofthemartyrs.com

Or write to:
FOTM, 118 N. Conistor, #B251, Liberty, MO 64068

You can see our other sites at:
www.TheChurchOfLiberty.com

We love you. May the Lord Jesus Christ richly bless you in whatever way He thinks best. (Which could include a 2x4 to the side of the head. But in love and just for your own good.)

APPENDIX A

WANNA HEAR THE VOICE OF GOD?

First, what exactly are we talking about? Does really God speak to people today?

Yes. In a whole bunch of ways from a gentle nudge, to instruction through the Bible, to using other people and circumstances to speak to you, to sending dreams and visions (or angels) – and/or even conversing directly with you.

You can hear God audibly and converse with Him?! You're kidding, right?

Not kidding. You can absolutely talk to God and He'll talk back. There are millions of people all over the world that rely on God for constant daily instruction on all sorts of things. But, there's a difference between hearing God audibly (with your natural ears, outside of your own head) and hearing the inner "still, small voice". It's pretty rare for God to speak to people audibly (like thunder), but there are plenty of folks out there that say they've heard Him – and the evidence is that once they did, it changed them forever! Many of the house churches in China are under such persecution that they can't set a regular time for meeting or even tell each other when the meeting will be – they all just pray and God Himself sets the time and place and tells each to be there. This is totally for real and the birthright of every believer!

Wait ... people hear the God of the Universe tell them stuff? Like what tie to wear and whether to turn left or right? What job to take? What to have for dinner? Not just big stuff?

Sure. The Bible says, "In all your ways acknowledge Him and He will direct your paths." (Prov. 3:5-6) What do you think "ALL your ways" means? And how is He going to direct you if you can't hear Him?

But my pastor said God doesn't talk to people like that!

Hmmm. Well, God used to talk to people all the time in the Bible. Wonder when He stopped? Did He say He was going to stop? Isn't He the same yesterday, today and forever? If anything, once the Holy Spirit came in Acts 2, there were LOTS more people talking to God directly! Never mind the MILLIONS of people who you have to conclude are thoroughly and certifiably nuts – including many of the most effective leaders of the church. In order to sustain that argument you have all kinds of logic problems.

Consider this:

IF God used to talk to people but doesn't now, THEN we must not need to hear from Him anymore. Can that be? By all measures we're worse off than ever. If there is a war between Good and Evil, we're losing pretty badly right now and really desperately need to be getting commands directly from Headquarters, not from flawed man-made sources and tradition-soaked interpretations of Scripture!

IF there is a battle between Good and Evil, THEN who would benefit most if the people on the "Good" side were told they couldn't ACTUALLY talk to their Commander in Chief? Now, you know the Evil side is absolutely clear to

EVERYONE that if you try to talk to THEIR leadership you WILL get an answer REAL fast! Even Christians are afraid to mess with Ouija boards and call on the names of demons because somewhere inside they believe something VERY real will show up almost instantly. But at the same time, the forces of darkness want us to buy that OUR God is mute! Doesn't that sound like something the snake would say in the Garden? Despite hundreds of examples in the Bible that He is available and accessible all the time, we have too often bought the lie that God is unwilling or unable to actually talk to His children. It's a lie from the pit and we've bought into it for too long.

IF we receive the Holy Spirit when we are saved, THEN 1/3 of the Godhead is living INSIDE of us all the time! (I John 4:13-17) But He doesn't have anything to say?! He's not interested in our daily activities? God's not big enough to know what we should have for lunch? He knows the hairs on our head and monitors our every coming and going, but has no opinion about it or desire to give us advice? What kind of Father is that?! IF we're dead and it's Christ in us that lives, THEN shouldn't HE be running the show? (Romans 7:4-6)

But my pastor says even HE doesn't hear God like that!

OK, well, you see, Matthew 18:18 says that, "what you bind on earth will be bound in heaven and what you loose on earth will be loosed in heaven." It goes on to say that if two of you on earth agree about anything you ask for, it will be done for you by the Father in heaven. (v. 19) So, could it be that we have whole groups of Christians that have agreed that God doesn't talk to people? And if they were convinced of that, don't those verses say that God will honor it? So maybe the problem is that if you're convinced God WON'T talk to you that way, He probably won't. And who would you blame? The pastor? Probably not – in fairness, we gotta lay it at the feet of the snake and the generations of tradition that have been built up to keep us from being truly "Spirit-led".

There could also be other problems that would keep a person from hearing God. One possibility is that they're on the wrong team - even if they think they're not. You know it's possible to make up your own "Jesus" and you'll get a response from that one about as good as if you were praying to a stick of wood. Another is that they have unrepented sin that stands between them and God – and God has convicted them of it so many times that He's just given up trying to talk to them.

Oh, and by the way, you're going to have to get over that thing about the pastor being more "holy" than you. This is a one-on-one relationship with Jesus you're supposed to have. You can't do it by proxy through the guy that gets paid to hear God (especially if he admits he's NOT hearing God!). We are ALL the Church. We are EACH temples that hold God's Spirit. Any one of us that are adopted sons of God have the ability to petition the Throne directly and seek His face. God loves each – in fact, He's especially fond of those that come to Him with faith like little children. Sometimes pastors have a hard time with that.

This is just crazy! How could this be true and I never knew it before? Wouldn't somebody have told me?

Well, I think you underestimate the damage the enemy has done and how long he's been plotting this. The vast majority of the church in the West doesn't live the "normal" Christian life. That is, Biblically speaking, we're to be full of power and might, we're to be free of the bondage of sin, we're to NOT conform to the world, we're to be dead to ourselves, we're to be ONE Body and loving and serving each other with all our heart. That's just a few. Can you see how far away from that we actually are as a "church"? We're not even CLOSE! There MUST be something missing. Somebody left something out! It has to be this – God is supposed to be directing you and you're supposed to be listening and OBEYING. Now ... who would benefit most from us leaving that little piece out? Yep, the guy in the black hat.

Now, what do you think a close encounter conversationally with the God of the Universe might do to a person? Trust me, it would change everything. It would show them the power of the relationship they have as adopted sons, they would lose all fear, they would sacrifice anything to keep hearing Him, they would obey and walk in HIS ways, they would know (really KNOW) that God Himself lives IN them and they would want more of Him, they would do the things on HIS heart – like feeding the hungry, clothing the naked, saving the lost. Probably would be a lot fewer chandeliers in the sanctuaries. (Probably be a lot fewer sanctuaries, for that matter.)

So, if this is a war between Good and Evil, wouldn't our most immediate and urgent need be to get people to where they can hear clear, timely, reliable commands from Headquarters? If you have a guy in Basic Training that refuses to listen to the Drill Sargeant and does his own thing, wouldn't you want to leave him at home? He's just going to get himself killed when the enemy starts shooting and leadership says 'DUCK!' and he can't or won't hear them. He's no good to anybody. Maybe he could be a supply clerk – but he really shouldn't be on the front lines.

But we have the Bible. God's word is what we are to use to direct our paths!

Ok, sure. Not got anything bad to say about the Bible! Everything God tells us to do will line up with the Bible. But no matter how well you know the Bible, it can't accommodate for every possible situation and what you should do. There's lots of stuff not covered in there – like which of these two jobs God wants me to take. And there's stuff in there that men have been arguing about for centuries without ever getting agreement. Lots of wasted time trying to figure out how many angels can dance on the head of a pin. (By the way, which side benefits most when God's people fight over stupid stuff? You getting the hang of this yet?)

Think of it like this. You're in the Army and they give you a Manual. All kinds of stuff is covered in there – what to wear, how to salute, how the weapons work, how to survive in a battle, what to eat in the forest, how the chain of command works, even what the enemy is like and how to resist them – there's even stuff in there about what the enemy WILL DO one day, whether they like it or not! It's a REALLY good Manual – in fact, it's inspired by God! It covers an amazing array of stuff and could probably handle most any situation. So would the Drill Sargeant ask you to read it, maybe even memorize it – and then send you into battle with nothing BUT that? Are you going to be able to know what to do when the bullets start flying? What about group strategy and deployment of forces and anticipating enemy movements? Is the Manual going to accommodate for every possible scenario on a rapidly changing battlefield? Are you sure you're interpreting it right? Is there time in the foxhole to be arguing with other soldiers that are reading it differently? What if some idiot published like TWENTY different translations and paraphrases of the Manual?! Then what?! Isn't there a chain of command? Isn't there somebody in charge calling the shots that's supposed to tell you what to do next?

Aren't you supposed to be listening and OBEYING? Want to go into battle without the Manual? No. Want to rely on it alone when you have other resources available? No. Want to take an order from somebody that goes against the Manual? No. When the bullets start flying, do you want to hear personally and directly from Headquarters so that you can know that help is coming or call in an air strike? You betcha!

I don't know. This is kind of scary. What if I hear wrong? What if it's the enemy messing with me? Maybe this is all in your mind.

Wow! That's a whole mess of stuff. Let's try this one at a time.

Maybe it's all in your mind.

Well, it's not just me. There's hundreds of millions like me that hear God. In fact, most of the growth in the Church worldwide is because of those people. The "mainline" denominations are shrinking. It's the Spirit-led revolutionaries that are exploding into new territories and pushing back the darkness.

Ok, let's try it from the opposite direction. It all sunk in for me one day when it struck me that satan never creates anything – he just makes weak copies of whatever God is doing. He's a liar and a deceiver and a fake. So ... while it may seem far-fetched, most folks (even Christians) will admit that evil is a real force in the world and the supernatural is real. (The Bible verifies repeatedly that witches and mediums and sorcery are real, by the way ... and that you're headed for hell if mess with them. – Deut 18:10-12, Col. 5:20) The enemy has psychics and mediums and astral projection and Ouija boards and demons and zombies and spells and curses.

So where's OUR stuff?! If this is a war, why does only one side get cool weapons? Was my church leaving out important stuff that I needed for warfare? Because in the first century they had amazing weapons and defenses available to them. They had the Holy Spirit telling them stuff they wouldn't have known (Acts 5:1-11), they had people hearing from God (Acts 13:2), they had people writing stuff as God dictated (Rev.), they were caught up in the Spirit to heaven (2 Corin. 12:2-4), they had dreams and visions (Acts 10:9-23), they saw angels (Acts 12), they saw Jesus Himself (Acts 9:1-22), they cast out demons (Acts 16:16-18), they were bitten by deadly snakes and didn't die (Acts 28:1-10), they spoke in other languages of men and of angels (Acts 2, I Corin. 12 & more), they healed people (Acts 5:15), they prayed and miracles happened (Acts 5:12, Acts 12) – even teleportation (or as we prefer – "theoportation" - Acts 8:39) and they raised the dead (Acts 9:32-42)! They even had people who were against them drop dead (Acts 5:1-11) or go blind (Acts 13:6-12) – on command! (And that's just ONE reference for each! There are lots more!)

Now, the argument is that all that ended when the Bible was done being written – but it didn't end for the other team, so how come just all OUR cool stuff got taken away? Wouldn't it have really benefited the enemy a LOT to spread that story around for a couple thousand years? Do you see? This is no kind of way to fight a war! There MUST be stuff we've been leaving out! The enemy has us twisted up into a thousand pieces (33,000+ denominations to be specific) and we can't STAND because we're not ONE Body. Because of all the arguing over stupid stuff – which we would NEVER have done if we had all been hearing the voice of God personally and reliably and walking in the Gifts!

This is kind of scary.

No kidding! It's the biggest thing ever in your life! That the God of the Universe wants to be intimately involved in everything you do and say and eat and wear and think. That's massively scary! And yet, we can never have peace and joy and victory until we have relationship with Jesus and are led by His Holy Spirit. You see, under our own power, we just screw everything up. There has never been any strategy of Man that has led to anything good in the long run. Oh, it might work for a little while, but you get enough sinful people involved in it, add money, mix in a little satan – and it's toast. Or worse, you get Communism or Fascism or something and millions of people die. There are just two options – if it's of Man it will fail and if it's of God nothing can stand against it. Since the "church" in America is failing, somebody other than God must be in charge. See a logic problem there?

Anyway, yes, it's scary. But what a payoff!! To walk in holiness because God Himself is fighting off the temptations and snares of the enemy, to hear Him all the time and get direction on anything and everything, to know that He is completely and totally in charge at all times in every situation. How are you going to find peace WITHOUT hearing from God? How is what you have NOW working for you?

And hearing His voice is not even a GIFT of the Spirit! It's just an automatic for every believer! We haven't even talked about prophecy and discernment of spirits and knowledge and wisdom and tongues and healing and all the other Gifts God gives His children! Trust me, the payoff is amazing, but it's going to cost you everything – but everything you THINK you have isn't yours anyway, so who cares!

What if the enemy is messing with me?

Well sure, that can happen. He's certainly going to try to confuse and frustrate you. We are specifically instructed, "do not believe every spirit, but test the spirits to see whether they are from God (1 John 4:1). That MUST mean that other spirits are potentially messing with us, and since there is no indication that this ended when the Bible was completed, then there must still be demons putting thoughts into our heads. And if there are still demons putting thoughts into our heads, then we must still have a need to test and see if they are from God. And if they're NOT from God, then we resist them and they flee. But it must also mean that one of the possibilities is that the spirit we're hearing IS from God! (Again, proving the point that God speaks to us.)

You see 1 John 4 goes on in verses 2 and 3 to lay out how you can know what it is that is talking to you and from where it comes, *"This is how you can recognize the Spirit of God: Every spirit that acknowledges that Jesus Christ has come in the flesh is from God, but every spirit that does not acknowledge Jesus is not from God. This is the spirit of the antichrist, which you have heard is coming and even now is already in the world."*

When we get a thought in our head we have to figure out who it is. There are only three choices: You, God or the enemy. Sometimes other people tell us stuff, but they're still playing to one of the three. We're to bring every thought into obedience with Christ (and the Bible). That means our own thoughts that are out of line AND the ones inserted by the enemy.

Could you screw it up? Sure. Particularly if the voices are VERY sneaky. Which they will be because demons are smarter than us and know the human condition very well after all these years of torturing and twisting us. Without God fighting for you, you haven't got a chance. You have to be constantly on guard, constantly armored-up and expecting anything from any direction.

OK. I'm getting that it's possible, but I'm going to have to hear Him for myself. I'm willing to try. What do we do?

Well the first thing is to ask the Lord to show you anything that stands in the way between you and Him. It's like this;

There is a pipeline of information that flows between us and God. He ALWAYS hears us, but if we can't hear Him, it is probably because of the things WE have put in the way.

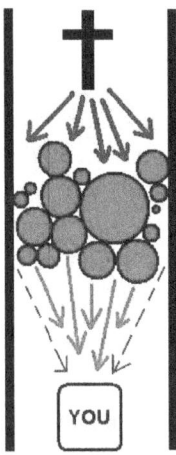 ANYTHING that we put between US and GOD is an idol. God never puts those things there. WE do. The most common thing is "religion" or the "pastor." Then ALL messages from God have to filter THROUGH that and get garbled. Others include sins and habits and addictions  and disobedience of one sort or another.

They ALL have to go. Only THEN can we get clear commands from Upstairs. Don't let ANYTHING come between you and God.

The point of the church coming together should be so that we can crucify pieces of ourselves so that Christ in us can live. Said another way, it's to help each other identify the things that stand between us and Jesus and pluck them out. The most common thing we put in the way is our belief that God won't talk to us. That's got to go! If you don't think He's a Living God and active and able to speak and desiring relationship with you, then you're going to have to lay that down. One of the other possibilities is that you're worshiping the WRONG Jesus. Paul said that would happen, that someone would come preaching another Jesus and people would accept it. It's very simple; if you make up your own Jesus, don't expect an answer when you pray! Prosperity-Jesus, Emergency-Only-Jesus, Lifeguard-Jesus, Not-Quite-As-Good-As-The-Virgin-Mary-Jesus, and a zillion others are all MADE UP. If you make your own god from scratch, expect about as much response as if you were praying to a stick. (Isaiah 44:6-20; Deuteronomy 4:28) Those are NOT Bible Jesus - who doesn't like to be toyed with and put in a box. Other things in the way are a reliance on someone else for your holiness or connection to God (Pastor, wife, mother, etc.). That's got to stop. This is a ONE-on-ONE relationship with Jesus you're supposed to be having. Nobody is going to do it for you. Other pipeline blockages include addiction, pride, selfishness, bitterness, anger, laziness, fear, love of money and so many others that keep us from experiencing the fullness that is IN Christ.

Ask the Lord to show you what is in the way and He is faithful to ALWAYS do that if you'll listen. Ask some other folks to pray with you if possible and just pray in agreement that the Lord will make Himself very clear to you about what to do next.

Here's another illustration that may help. We all have a cup. Lots of verses in the Bible about that - jars of clay, wineskins, vessels, vials, bottles, bowls, etc. So the question is, "What's in your cup?"

How the Cups work:

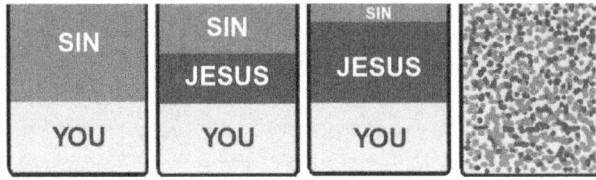

Because of our fallen nature and the fact that satan owns us, we all start out with just "Us" and "Sin" in our cups. At some point, if we're lucky, we get "saved" - which really just means we admit we need God and He stands in the gap between YOU and SIN and starts telling you to get it out of there. The "World" is always working to foil the plans of God. Since they can't snatch YOU out of the hand of Jesus, the enemy just neutralizes us by keeping us a constant slave to sin. The best method is to shake the whole thing up like vinaigrette so you can't slow down long enough to figure out what's really wrong. Ever feel shook up like that?

What prayer is for is to settle out the layers real fast. If you hear the Holy Spirit and obey, you'll displace the SIN with more God. If you can be so full of Jesus that nothing else will fit anymore, then you can displace the SIN. But this is a DAILY thing, not once and for all. He's our Daily Bread. We need to be full of Jesus all the time.

But if you can get the (red) Sin stuff at the top out, the

Bible says "The steps of a righteous man are ordered before him." So He'll start running your life for you. Which is better anyway, because the yellow YOU in your cup really has no idea what it's doing. Eventually the Holy Spirit will look at the YOU in your cup and start pouring that out, too! If you can walk in it and be a good steward, He'll give you a bigger cup full of Him (expand your territory, extend your tent, etc.). Then, even if there's just as much of YOU as before, there's lots more of HIM, so the balance of power starts shifting more and more. If you want your SHADOW to heal people like Peter's in Acts, you better have a cup like an oil tanker and it better be full of Jesus (the blue part)!

If the prayer of a righteous man availeth much, the prayer of a "slightly righteous" man availeth practically nothing. If you're not being obedient to HIM, why is HE going to answer your prayers? If there's red stuff in your cup, He's only interested in hearing ONE thing from you -- "I repent, Lord. Please fill me with Your Spirit." That's what happened in Acts 2. They got great big cups full of Jesus.

That's ALWAYS inside His will. Can you pray that and mean it? If you do, I have NO idea what will happen. He could send you to Africa, He could make you speak in other languages, your shadow could start healing people -- I have NO idea. But I know He's a good Father and He won't give us a stone when we ask for bread. You CANNOT seek the Holy Spirit with a pure heart and something else sneak in there instead. The very foremost thing on God's heart is for you to be full of Him. There is no peace and joy and victory without that.

Just pray and believe. He'll come.

More on the cups and how to keep your cup so jammed, packed full of Jesus that nothing else can fit here -

www.FellowshipOfTheMartyrs.com/rain_right_now.htm

Lots more resources and materials about personal growth, the church, the Holy Spirit and more on our site.

www.FellowshipOfTheMartyrs.com

APPENDIX B

STRAIGHT TALK ABOUT SPEAKING IN TONGUES

First, you have to understand that I was born and bred a staunch Southern Baptist. Son of a pastor and missionaries. Got degrees in religion and psychology from an SBC college. I understand how the brain can be used to mess with you. I understand about mind control and subconscious programming - AND I understand about witchcraft and demonic controls. I'm a business man and a pragmatist. I'm just not the rolling around on the floor kind of a guy. I just don't go in for theatrics. I want NOTHING that isn't PURE Jesus.

But I've learned a lot in the last couple of years as the Holy Spirit has taken me on this wild adventure to unlearn layers and layers of stuff that I was taught and relearn them the way He wanted. In the last year and half, I've had the great priviledge to fellowship with more than fifty different congregations of all different flavors. And I can state unequivocally that they ALL see through a glass darkly! No question about it. If they think they don't, it's because their vision is blurred by the big pride plank in their eye. But they all see through different PARTS of the glass darkly. That is, some are clear about Sin and some aren't. Some are clear about Gifts and some aren't. Some are clear about the Holy Spirit and some aren't. Some are right on the substance, but not the application. Because the Body of Christ is divided into 37,000+ denominations that aren't talking to each other, we can't get a coherent picture of the totality of Christ. Like putting together a puzzle without the picture on the box.

What I do is synthesize and congeal all the different stuff I've seen across the whole of the Body of Christ to see if I can get an approximation of the picture on the box.

As that relates to tongues (and other "manifestation" gifts of the Spirit), here is my take on this, for what it's worth.

First, the gifts are not On/Off switches, they are dials. That's really important because so many people think that you either speak in tongues or you don't and if you don't then you haven't received the Baptism of the Holy Spirit. Some even believe that you're not going to heaven unless you speak in tongues. But I've met LOTS of people that speak in tongues and hardly ANY of them received the Baptism of Fire described in Luke 3:16. Hardly anybody is really walking in holiness and sanctification. So they're not obeying and they shouldn't be so comfy in their sense that because they speak in tongues, they're FULL of the Holy Spirit and therefore safe. I know some serious sinners that speak in tongues. It's a GIFT, and that means He'll probably let you keep it, even if you're a backslidden stinker.

People ask me if I'm "Spirit-Filled". I ask them, "Do you mean that at some point I had an experience with God and spoke in tongues or that I'm so crammed full of the Holy Spirit all the time that nothing else can fit? Cause it ain't the same thing." We're to "be being filled". Not a one time thing. If you pray for JUST enough Holy Spirit to speak in tongues, you just might get a little shot glass full of the Holy Spirit. If you pray for Wisdom and Sanctification and let God work the rest of the gifts out with you in His time, you'll probably get a GREAT BIG cup of the Holy Spirit and He'll teach you how to keep it full. And you'll probably get a whole bunch of the gifts, not just tongues. If you don't have, it's because you don't ask.

Anyway, back to the issue at hand. I had to get an understanding about the difference between a prophetic message given in tongues in front of the church (which should be interpreted) and a personal "prayer language" that you would use when you're alone. Some folks say that tongues are for the edification of the Body, therefore should never be done in private since there is no one there to interpret. But Paul says when he prays in tongues he is edified personally, even if nobody else is around. And since I need all the edifying I can get, well then I might as well ask for all the gifts that will help!

Why does it edify you to pray in tongues, even if you don't understand what you're saying? It's really very simple - you see, the Holy Spirit is praying FOR you. And He knows EXACTLY what you need. He's very efficient, so a lot of praying can get done in a lot shorter amount of time. The added benefit is that when the Spirit prays it's like an encrypted transmission to the throne that the enemy can't intercept and mess with. If you pray in English (or your native language) for peace or strength or for a person that's on your heart, the enemy hears it and will probably do what he can to dial up the pressure on those areas so that your prayers don't seem answered. And, when you pray in tongues, the enemy really, really doesn't like being around it. You can clear all the badness out of your house by just walking around it and praying in the Spirit. Some people sing in tongues and the Spirit writes the melody and gives them the words - and sometimes the interpretation. It's really pretty when it's pure!

When the Spirit prays, it may not be for a decision about your job or a new car - it may be for a gifting or a call or for divine appointments or the stranger on the bus or something you wouldn't even think to pray. Sometimes the Holy Spirit doesn't even use words. Sometimes all that can come out is groaning or crying or mournful screaming in pain. Those are just some of the various flavors of how the Spirit can pray through you.

It's like this. If the Holy Spirit is in you - which He is from the moment you commit your life to follow Jesus - then He can pray FOR you THROUGH you if you'll just get out of the way. Although it wasn't until November 23, 2004 that I had a personal experience of the "Baptism with the Spirit and with Fire" variety, I can think of many times over the decades previous when I would be on my face praying and crying with a huge burden on my heart and nothing but groans would come out. In fact, nearly every Christian I've spoken with that really loves Jesus, whether Baptist, Methodist, Presbyterian or otherwise can remember times after they got "saved" when they were praying and something else seemed to just take over or help them pray. Not that a language came out necessarily, but maybe just a deep moan from the pit of their stomach but they knew it was God. In know some people that pray in English, but it's not really them praying anymore. Or some that just weep when they intercede for others. I don't care what any charismatic says, that's "tongues" and it counts. Which means you had it BEFORE somebody laid hands on you to receive the "Baptism" - which means it's NOT an On/Off switch, it's a DIAL and everybody that has the Holy Spirit is automatically NOT on Zero.

After my experience with God and the vision He gave me and the mission He launched me into, because of the burden He put on me, that deep groaning was all that I could get out when I was praying. Since then, I've learned to recognize and get out of the way of all the other "flavors" that the Holy Spirit might use to pray through me -

including a variety of languages of Man (with or without personal interpretation), sometimes just tears, sometimes screaming and wailing, sometimes just a deep sigh. But I can tell the difference whether it's the Holy Spirit or just me, and when it's Him, then that's what you call "Praying in the Spirit." And from God's perspective they are all linguistic. He understands the "words of our groaning." (Psalm 22:1)

The short of this is that I believe that when you first receive ANY of the Holy Spirit, your "tongues" dial (and the other ones) turns from ZERO to whatever He wants to put it on. If you want more and ask for it, He'll dial it up and you may get something instantly or over time or of any of a huge variety of flavors. Basically, the more transparent you are - the more you get out of the way - the more the Holy Spirit can do whatever He wants through you and the more dangerous you are to the enemy. The more you seek Him and get out of His way, the higher your dial gets turned.

Now, you still have to test the spirits. Don't get me wrong. I'm not in favor of chicken clucking or airplane sounds. You don't want to do anything out of your own flesh or to imitate someone else just to fit in! That's just mocking God. Essentially, you're taking the Lord's name in vain when you "fake" tongues or use it outside of His guidelines. Or when you don't test the spirits and allow something bad to get in so you can have an "experience".

There are satanists and witches that can speak in all kinds of tongues. Demons know all the languages of Man so it's no big deal for them to influence someone that is receptive. Hearing someone speak in tongues is NO evidence that God is in them! Without the gift of discernment of spirits or hearing God really well and asking Him specifically about someone, you are pretty much flying blind to know if it's from God or not in someone else. You should watch for the fruit, but sometimes in a public meeting with strangers there's no way to see that. I've personally dealt with demonic tongues on multiple occasions in Christians who didn't know it wasn't from God. But someone they didn't know laid hands on them and gave them something icky (and they allowed it or sought it). Always ask the Lord to guard you with the Blood of Jesus against anything bad coming from anybody that would lay hands on you!

So, to summarize, why pray in your own strength when you could just get out of the way and let the Holy Spirit pray THROUGH you? Isn't it just prideful in the extreme that you think you can pray better than the THIRD of the Godhead that lives in you?! If you have Jesus, you can pray in the Spirit. Just ask Him to teach you how and believe that He wants to. You don't need some big showy huddle down front at the church with lots of people praying on you and shaking you. Just ask in faith and believe that He wants you to learn how to pray in the most efficient possible way. He's a good Dad. He's not going to give you a stone if you ask for bread.

I can tell you, my walk with God hit warp speed when I started letting Him pray for me! Now I spend anywhere from four to eight hours a day praying in the Spirit (in one form or another as He leads). And since the Spirit is praying, my mind is idle, so I can go about my business or drive or pray in my mind for something else. It's like double-barrel praying! (I Corin. 14:14-15)

There are those that say that tongues are dead and it's not for today. They are insulting and demeaning and marginalizing the deep, daily experience of about 800,000,000+ Jesus-lovers all around the world. They are calling brothers and sisters in Christ liars and cheats and/or unstable tools of satan. They are saying that - since

He did something THEN that He doesn't do now and made a promise that it was for us, but didn't mean it – then God changes and the Bible is not reliable. Since the VAST majority of growth in the church world-wide is because of the tongue-speaking charismatic arm of the spectrum, those who are staunchly entrenched in their mainline, fundamental denominations are really arguing from a losing position. If they're really going to put their money where their mouth is, then they should scrub out of their lives EVERY tongue-speaking preacher, musician, missionary, theologian, teacher, writer, etc. And since they would be left with VERY little music, art, literature, radio or TV and practically no effective missions efforts locally and abroad, they probably need to rethink their devise ways. Maybe reread Galatians 5:19-21 (especially that part about strife and division and not inheriting the Kingdom of Heaven).

There are those that say "tongues" (glossolalia is the technical term) are indeed a real manifestation of God and MIGHT be for today but they are ONLY languages of Man used in public for evangelization - and since there is no evidence whatsover of ANYONE speaking in a language of Man in the last 1900+ years, then it's not for today." This statement is a giant crock of dog doodie. It is a bold faced lie and is uneducated and uninformed and unresearched. I am personally familiar with people that have prayed in tongues and been told by others present that it was perfect Japanese. I'm aware of two people in other countries that had an urgent need and prayed and God gave them ENGLISH! I'm aware of Wycliffe Bible Translators deep in a jungle somewhere who have the Lord give them a prayer language to help reach the people group they're working with. The 1901 Pentecostal renewal that started with Parham's Bible school in Topeka, KS showed documented evidence by newspaper reporters of his students spontaneously speaking in dozens of languages of other countries that were previously unknown to them. At the Azusa Street Revival in 1906 to 1909 there were hundreds of documented cases of people speaking, writing and singing in, unknown to them but known to others present, or documentable languages. There is evidence throughout church history of outbreaks of tongues for specific evangelistic purposes to overcome language barriers.

Further, I think that is our ONLY hope of reaching all people groups with the Gospel anytime soon, since the process of learning and translating the Bible into the remaining thousands of dialects is going to take a REALLY long time at our current rate of spending. Do some research. God is still alive and moving. He established the language barriers at Babel, He can remove them anytime He wants. And He is still doing it all over the world, all the time. He can do it through and in you if you will let Him.

Don't be afraid of God. He knows what He's doing. He's not going to give you a stone when you pray for bread. Just ask and believe in faith it's possible. Stop putting Him in a box. Just get out of the way and let Him be God.

If it helps, pray this:

> Lord, if there is more out there that you have for me than I realize, would you please reveal it to me? I want to be effective in my prayer life and I want to be closer with You. I want to hear Your voice and have the kind of intimacy that David and Paul and Moses and Jesus had. I want to hear you clearly. Please let Your Holy Spirit flow through me in whatever way You think best. Teach me how to pray. I love You and I trust You. Do it however You like ... but right NOW would be nice. In the Name of Jesus I send this petition to the Father, knowing it's inside Your will and that You WILL answer it. Amen.

APPENDIX C

ARE YOU SURE YOU'RE NOT NUTS?

Boy, I'll tell you what! Sometimes I read over stuff like this that I have written and the Missouri Show-Me, Southern Baptist preacher's kid in me does sort of wonder if I'm nuts. But the Bible is clear, we are spiritual beings temporarily trapped in jars of clay. We are to walk in the spirit, not focus on the flesh. Our battle is NOT against flesh and blood, but against powers and principalities and wickedness in high places and the dark forces of this world. Neither is our battle to be done WITH our flesh and blood. Our spirit (or rather His in us) is where our true power rests.

So, yeah, this seems really supernatural and mystical to me sometimes, except that God has proven it to me so many times that I couldn't even begin to count. I've seen demons (in the spirit) on someone and reached out and grabbed them and ripped them off and they quit smoking or are healed of Autism or their pain stops instantly or they don't need their schizophrenia medicine anymore. Over and over and over. And I've seen people (strong Christians!) be unable or unwilling to keep the doors shut and it comes back seven times worse and within HOURS they're beating their wife and doing drugs and cursing me out – or worse! I know demons are real because the Lord has proven it to me over and over and I've seen what they do, how they act, where they hide, how to get rid of them, how they come back, how they work together and more.

There is a certain segment of the "church" that will insult and demean anything that is "supernatural" and yet they gather together to pray on Wednesday nights for the sick people in their churches. They pray that the doctors would have wisdom, that their recovery would be slightly faster than normal, that they would have peace with the sickness that the Lord has placed on them. Hogwash! What kind of power is that? What kind of inheritance? If you don't believe God heals, then why pray at all? Why not just write a note of encouragement to their doctor? If you just sit around and send out good vibes to their doctor, how is that not a form of New Age meditation? Where in the Bible does it say to go to a doctor anyway? Who is the Great Physician? What doctor can heal if God doesn't want someone healed? What doctor can save a life that God wants to take? And who can kill someone God wants to keep alive? How many examples do you want of people that I know that are unkillable? I have a friend that tried to commit suicide so many times and kept getting saved by angels that finally an angel came and said, "Would you just KNOCK IT OFF! We're never going to let you kill yourself!" And that was BEFORE he came to Jesus! If God has something for you to do, until you do it, you're indestructible! Why be afraid of Man? And if God wants you dead, NOBODY can save you. Be afraid of God.

Oops! Sorry, started preaching again. Anyway ...

Those sections of the church that deny that the Gifts of the Spirit are for today are still brothers and sisters and I love them. But they're not going to be very much help fighting a war in the spirit with weapons they say aren't real and against an enemy they insist isn't there. Some even believe that God doesn't speak to people anymore. What kind of a war is that? In the meantime, their churches are full of sick, shackled, addicted, fearful, obese people with no peace and joy and victory. They have the appearance of Christ, but deny the power thereof. That can't be good. But I love them and want them to come around. It's not the people's fault, it's the doctrines of man jammed down their throat by seminarians who will not back down from the status quo. But I think God is coming in power real soon and He's going to settle the issue once and for all.

Yes, there are lying signs and wonders already and many more coming. There are false prophets that heal and deliver people of demons (or seem to). But the fact that satan has cheap imitations DOES NOT negate the originals! Who benefits most if God does supernatural stuff and satan does supernatural stuff, but you dismiss them BOTH because ONE of them was from satan? Don't you think that's going to irritate God – to constantly be told that anything supernatural that He does was actually the work of satan? I mean how can God do anything that's NOT supernatural – by definition, He's not "natural"! When God equips someone with faith and power and they take the Bible seriously and go out and fulfill the Great Commission as it's written at the end of the Gospel of Mark and people keep saying they are tools of satan, don't you think that's going to irritate God?

Whatever else I may be, I've got peace and joy and victory and I'm deliriously happy. If the voice I'm hearing is NOT God, then it sure sounds like Him and He keeps telling me to do stuff that you would think would really, really make satan mad. If this voice isn't really God, I don't care, I'm gonna stick with it until this whole ride plays out to the end. I'm going to bet on radical obedience and a pure heart being a really good thing (heavenly treasure-wise) and if I go down, I'm going down swinging for the fences. God will judge my heart, not the perfection and purity of my doctrine. He wants faith like a child, not faith like a belligerent teenager.

APPENDIX D

Open Letter of Apology to The World

from Doug Perry, February 2005

Please bear with me, this is long overdue and there's lots of ground to cover. I want to make sure that I get it all out. Not just for me, but because I think you need to hear it. Maybe there are other Christians out there as well that need to make apologies and will find courage here. I appreciate your time, I know it's valuable.

Dear Members of the World,

I'm just a guy, nobody really. Son of a preacher and missionary. Years and years of Vacation Bible Schools, summer camps, youth ski trips, puppet shows, revivals, choir trips - you name it. Even went to a Christian college and got a degree in religion. I ended up in the business world, but I spent two decades tithing, sitting on committees, teaching Sunday School, going to seminars and conferences, etc. I even met my wife in the single's class at church. I'm not a bad guy, I've been mostly behaving myself and everybody seems to like me. I do some good stuff here and there.

But lately I've been trying to understand Jesus more and stuff I never noticed before has really started to bug me. I've been taking a look around and I'm having a hard time making sense of what it is we've built here. So, it just seemed like, whether anybody else says it or not, I need to take responsibility for the part I played and say what I have to say.

Here we go ...

I know you think that Christians are a big bunch of hypocrites. We say we're more "religious" and we're going to heaven and you're not, and then we drive our big shiny cars with little fishies on the trunk and cut you off in traffic as we race by the homeless guy on the corner. We average just 2% of our money to church and charity, despite that we say the Bible is the word of God and **it** says we're supposed to give **everything**. On average, we buy just as many big screen TVs and bass boats and fur coats and makeup and baseball cards and online porn as anybody else. Maybe more. You've seen leader after leader end up in jail or court or a sex scandal of one sort or another.

Well ... you're right. We're guilty of all of it. We've done it all. And, I'm really sorry.

You see our cheesy TV shows and slick guys begging for money and you get that there's something seriously sneaky and wrong here. A high-pressure call for money so they can stay on the air? Were we supposed to use Jesus as just another form of entertainment? Who do we think we're kidding? Where's Jesus in all this? Aren't we supposed to rely on him? Isn't He going to meet our needs if we're inside His will?

What happened to sacrifice and suffering and helping the poor? I'm just sick about this. I mean, the church leaders, they're not all bad guys, there are lots and lots of really hard-working well-meaning folks who love and care and are meeting real needs in the community. Some of them understand and love Jesus - but I'm just real sure those pastors don't drive Bentley's, have multi-million dollar homes and their own lear jets! I mean, what "god" are we worshipping? Money? Ego? Power?

You see our massive shiny new buildings all over the place. Heck, maybe we even kicked you out of your house so we could expand our parking lots. You can't figure out why we need four different Christian churches on four corners of the same intersection. We've got playgrounds and bowling alleys and basketball leagues. We've got Starbucks coffee in the sanctuary. We've got orchestras and giant chandeliers and fountains out front. We've got bookstores full of "jesus junk" with every imaginable style and flavor of religious knick-knack. But where's Jesus? Is this what HE wanted?

Oh, sure, there are good folks all over and not every church is such a mess, but Christians are the ones that say we're supposed to be "One Body." So even the good ones are guilty of not putting a stop to it sooner. We were supposed to keep each other in line and not tolerate factions and dissensions and greed and idolatry and all this other bad stuff. Man, we really blew it! We've got 33,000 denominations and most of them won't talk to the other ones. We lose over $5 million a day to fraud from "trusted" people inside the church! We spend 95% of all our money on our own comforts and programs and happy family fun time shows and we let 250 MILLION Christians in other countries live on the very edge of starvation. Not to mention the billion or so that have never even once heard of Jesus - or the homeless guy downtown we almost ran over when we cut you off.

We're as guilty as we can be. All of us. Nobody is exempt. We should have put a stop to it a lot sooner. But I can't apologize on behalf of anyone else. This is about me.

I know that you might have gone to church as a kid and stopped going as soon as you could. I know that you might even have been abused by somebody in the church! Maybe we got you all fired up and then just let you drift off like we didn't really care. Maybe you just don't fit our "profile." You might have piercings and purple hair or tattoos or been in jail -- and somewhere inside you just know that even if you wanted to go to church one Sunday, it would not go well. I'm sorry for that. Jesus loves you. He always hung out with the most unexpected people. He had the biggest heart for the folks everybody else tried to ignore. What have we done? We've told you to put on a sweater and some loafers or you can't go to heaven. I just want to throw up.

Look, I know you're mad. And you have a right to be. We've done you wrong for a LONG time now. There's some things about Jesus that people need to hear, but we've buried a beautiful masterpiece under hundreds of layers of soft pink latex paint. If you have a Bible handy, look up Matthew 23. (If you don't, you can look it up here - www.BibleGateway.com .)

Find it? Read it carefully, the Pharisees were the "religious" people of the day, the leaders of the faith. In this chapter Jesus SEVEN times says how pitiful and wretched and cursed they are for what they're doing to the people they're supposed to be leading. He even calls them "white washed tombs of dead mens bones" and a "brood of vipers"! I don't have time here, but read it and see if we're not doing EVERY single one of those things. Jesus can't possibly be happy about what we've done to you.

Sure, we like to kid ourselves and pretend everything is OK - but it's not. We're hated. Now, please understand, Jesus was hated, too. But that was because he said hard things and sometimes people don't like hearing the Truth. And he promised we would be hated if we were like him. But that's not why we're hated at the moment. We're hated right now because we're a giant pack of lying hypocrites that say one thing and do something else altogether. If we were hated because we were like Jesus, that would be one thing, but that's not it at all. You see right through our happy music and fluffy services and you can tell there's something desperately wrong here. We're no different than anybody else - except that we say we're better than you.

It was never supposed to be like this. Jesus asked us to care for the widows and orphans, to feed the hungry, care for the sick, visit those in prison, reach the lost. He wanted us to love our enemies and pray for them. He cared about human justice and suffering, the lost and lonely. But I don't think He would have marched on a picket line - He had His mind on much bigger problems. He wanted us to focus on the eternal things, not the everyday. He never once said to go into all the world and build big buildings and divide up into factions and buy Bentleys. Just the opposite! I get that you're mad at us and I think you have a right to be, but please understand, you're mad at what we've made under our own power, you're mad at "Churchianity." That's different than Christ and what he wanted. Don't be mad at Jesus! This mess wasn't His idea!

Look, I'm really sorry. I accept responsibility for my part in having hurt you. But I'm committing to you all, dear Members of the World, that I'm not going to do it any more. Not a single penny more. I'm not going to put my faith in "Churchianity" or any leader or program or TV show -- but in Christ Jesus and His salvation. That's when I was set free and began to see that God wants and expects more of us than this. And I'm not helping anybody that's not fully committed to the same thing.

It took centuries to build this monster, so it's not like it's going to just turn around overnight. But the times are changing and we're way overdue for something new. Big bad things are happening - like the tsunami in Asia - and I think more are coming. I don't want any more time to go by without having said this. I'm sorry for all the time and money I've wasted. But Jesus saves. Really. The church itself isn't even the point. Jesus is the real deal. He lived and He died for my sins and He rose again. He is who He said He was and He cares about me - and you. He's our only hope. We need places you can go that will only teach Jesus and will not be swayed or tempted or distracted by anything else. God willing, that's coming.

Please don't think all Christians are just posers. Some of them really mean it when they say they belong to Christ. The problem is mostly in the West where we're all comfy and complacent and seem to like it that way. The Christians in China and other places are deadly serious. There's no room for anything but Jesus when you're on the run from the government. They are dying every day for their faith and doing crazy hard things because they're absolutely committed to Christ. These are martyrs. People willing to crucify little pieces of themselves every day to be more like Christ. People willing to set aside everything they want, to do what Christ wants. People willing to rot in prison or take a beating or die if that's what it's going to take. People that act in pure love and never back down. I'm not worthy to tie their shoes. And there are some like that here, too, and I hope we can get a lot more people to start living that way. It's way overdue.

If you're talking to someone and they tell you they're a Christian, ask them if they're the kind of Christian that really means it all the time or the kind that just means it on Sunday. The Bible says we'll know them by their "fruits" - by the faith and purity and love in their deeds and words. When you find one that proves Christ is in them by how much they love you, ask them to tell you all about Jesus. If you know one of those fearless martyrs that speaks nothing but pure, clean, hard Truth - ask lots of questions. Truth is a lot more rare than you would think. But don't settle for soft, fluffy and comfortable anymore - that's not in the Bible.

As for me and my house, we're really sorry. From now on, we're going to serve the Lord, not "Churchianity." We're going to try to call together as many of those martyrs as we can and start doing what Christ wanted. If I run into you someday, please give me a chance to shake your hand and apologize in person. I'm going to try harder from now on, I promise. I think there are lots of others feeling the same way, so don't be surprised if you start hearing stuff like this more often.

Thanks for your time. I hope it helps.

Doug Perry

from the Church in Liberty, Missouri
www.TheChurchOfLiberty.com
help@thechurchofliberty.com

Use freely, but without changes or removing attribution.

ABOUT THE AUTHOR

Doug Perry has been going 200 miles an hour with his hair on fire since November 23, 2004 when God showed him an open vision of how much God loves His children, how angry God is for how we're killing His children, and how much we have to hurry. It's safe to say that praying to see through the eyes of Jesus and be dangerous to satan wrecked his life. He had a nice home, a wife, two kids, two dogs, a foreign car with a sunroof, and a multimillion dollar, award-winning business that was named the #4 fastest growing company in Kansas City in 2005. He was even teaching Sunday School.

Then he realized what he was, what we've built, and how it looks in the light of holiness. He realized he was a friend of the world – and an enemy of God. (James 4:4) So he sold all he had and gave it to the poor – or it was stripped from him one way or another. And it was all worth it.

Now he's the author of seven books, nearly a thousand videos, music, poetry, and founder of a homeless shelter and a food pantry that feeds 5,000+ people every month. He has cried on the sidewalk in public for days. He's been arrested on false charges. He's spent weeks at a time in prayer, fasting and weeping for the sad state of things.

And he's been spit on, lied about, abandoned, forsaken by friends, banned by pastors, ejected from sanctuaries – and looks more like Jesus all the time. He's even had people try to physically kill him! Just for speaking the hard truth nobody wants to hear. But Jesus said it would be like that. Praise God! Bring it on.

If nobody is shooting at you, then you're _not_ dangerous.

OTHER TITLES FROM FELLOWSHIP OF THE MARTYRS PUBLISHING

Rain Right *NOW*, Lord! - from Doug Perry
What is it going to take for God to pour His Spirit out on all flesh? Or is He waiting for us? Are spiritual gifts real and for today – and how do you get more of them?

The Apology to the World – from Doug Perry
The "Apology to the World" letter has influenced thousands and been all over the world. This book spawned from responses to that letter and collected writings about the need for change.

Left-Handed Warriors – from Linda Carriger
A suspenseful tale of the supernatural vs. the natural. What was it like for kids growing up in the book of Acts? Linda paints a picture of what it's like to be radically sold out to Christ – and still a kid.

Missionaries are Human, Too – from Nancy Perry
A sweet, candid look at what it's like to be a missionary family learning to trust God in a foreign country. (1976)

Dialogues With God – from Doug Perry
Some discussions between Doug and the Almighty, along with a trouble-shooting guide to help you get unclogged, get your cup full and hear God better.

DEMONS?! You're kidding, right? - from Doug Perry
A very detailed guide to spiritual warfare – how the bad guys act, what they look like, where they hide and much more. For experts only. Not for sissies. Seriously. We're not kidding.

Do It Yourself City Church Restoration – Doug Perry
What was 'church' supposed to be like all along? Are we doing it right? What's it going to take to fix it? If Jesus Christ wrote a letter to the Body of Christ in your city, could you bear to read it? What would happen if you were One Body in your town?

Who Neutered the Holy Spirit?! - from **Doug Perry**
Why do people say that the Holy Spirit stopped doing all the cool stuff that used to happen? This details the scriptural evidence of the work of the Spirit in the Old Testament, in the New Testament, after Pentecost, and in the church today. Along with help to get you unclogged so you can walk in the fullness of what God has for you.

The Red Dragon: the horrifying truth about why the 'church' cannot seem to change – from **Doug Perry**
How bad are things? How did they get this bad? In fact, they're SO bad, they have to be considered supernaturally bad! In fact, it's a curse from God. A delusion sent on those that went their own way. Weep. No really, weep! That's your only hope.

Expelling Xavier – from **Dorothy Haile**
A love story between a girl possessed by something dark and a boy just learning who he is in Christ – and their Savior. A very different kind of Christian novel, gritty, rough and fiercely transparent about the realities of life under the control of the darkness.

Fellowship Of The Martyrs Volume 1 – from **Doug Perry**
One mega book combining:
> The Apology to the World
> The Red Dragon
> Dialogues with God
> Rain Right NOW, Lord!
> Do It Yourself City Church Restoration

A compete course; from what's wrong with the church, how to fix YOU first, how to get your cup full and get big and strong and then how to bring real revival and restore the manifestation of "church" in your town as it was always meant to be.

And LOTS more titles coming soon!!
And in SPANISH!

Made in the USA
Monee, IL
17 March 2023